T0294854

Harnessing Mobile Technology to Enable U.S. Personnel Vetting

DAVID STEBBINS, SARAH W. DENTON, DOUGLAS YEUNG

Prepared for the Performance Accountability Council Program Management Office
Approved for public release; distribution unlimited

NATIONAL DEFENSE RESEARCH INSTITUTE

For more information on this publication, visit **www.rand.org/t/RRA1689-1**.

About RAND

The RAND Corporation is a research organization that develops solutions to public policy challenges to help make communities throughout the world safer and more secure, healthier and more prosperous. RAND is nonprofit, nonpartisan, and committed to the public interest. To learn more about RAND, visit www.rand.org.

Research Integrity

Our mission to help improve policy and decisionmaking through research and analysis is enabled through our core values of quality and objectivity and our unwavering commitment to the highest level of integrity and ethical behavior. To help ensure our research and analysis are rigorous, objective, and nonpartisan, we subject our research publications to a robust and exacting quality-assurance process; avoid both the appearance and reality of financial and other conflicts of interest through staff training, project screening, and a policy of mandatory disclosure; and pursue transparency in our research engagements through our commitment to the open publication of our research findings and recommendations, disclosure of the source of funding of published research, and policies to ensure intellectual independence. For more information, visit www.rand.org/about/research-integrity.

RAND's publications do not necessarily reflect the opinions of its research clients and sponsors.

Published by the RAND Corporation, Santa Monica, Calif.
© 2023 RAND Corporation
RAND® is a registered trademark.

Library of Congress Cataloging-in-Publication Data is available for this publication.

ISBN: 978-1-9774-1017-7

Cover: Mangostar/Adobe Stock.

About This Report

Global pandemic conditions fundamentally altered every aspect of the U.S. government's (USG's) hiring and screening model. Coronavirus disease 2019 (COVID-19) operating conditions disrupted traditional in-person and paper-based USG vetting methods developed more than 70 years ago.[1] Organizations responsible for vetting prospective government employees modified existing security, suitability, and credentialing (SSC) processes to accommodate changes in line with sociocultural shifts to the hybrid and virtual working environments. The move to a mobile hiring and screening process faces several challenges. Longstanding institutional norms and a well-established security vetting culture may be the most significant obstacles to full mobile screening implementation.

This exploratory research report examines how the USG might use mobile and other virtual technologies in pre-onboarding stages to enable overall efficiencies within the SSC process and within the context of the Trusted Workforce (TW) 2.0 initiative.[2] The research, findings, and suggestions that appear throughout this report are derived from several sources, including interviews with organizations in the private sector, some of which pioneered use of mobile and virtual technologies even prior to the pandemic onset.

The research reported here was completed in September 2022 and underwent security review with the sponsor and the Defense Office of Prepublication and Security Review before public release.

This research was sponsored by the Performance Accountability Council Program Management Office (PAC PMO) and conducted within the Forces and Resources Policy Center of the RAND National Security Research Division (NSRD), which operates the National Defense Research Institute (NDRI), a federally funded research and development program sponsored by the Office of the Secretary of Defense, the Joint Staff, the Unified Combatant Commands, the Navy, the Marine Corps, the defense agencies, and the defense intelligence enterprise.

For more information on the RAND Forces and Resources Policy Center, see www.rand.org/nsrd/frp or contact the director (contact information is provided on the webpage).

Acknowledgments

The research contained within this report would not have been possible without the input, assistance, and continued support from several individuals. We would like to thank David

---

[1] The security clearance process was formalized through the 1947 National Security Act (Public Law 235, National Security Act of 1947, July 26, 1947).

[2] We discuss the TW initiative below.

Colangelo, Heather Clawson, and Renee Oberlin at the PAC PMO (our sponsoring office) for their continuous guidance, feedback, and suggestions for our interviews with USG personnel. We would like to express our gratitude to the private-sector subject-matter experts (SMEs) and technology vendors we spoke with over the course of this project, who informed many of the findings and suggestions that appear in this report. We would also like to take this opportunity to thank the personnel vetting, human resources, and legal SME participants in our SME workshop. Finally, we would like to thank our reviewers, Sina Beaghley, Ginger Groeber, and Daniel Ginsberg, for their thoughtful review of this report.

Summary

This applied research project provides the Security, Suitability, and Credentialing (SSC) Performance Accountability Council Program Management Office (PAC PMO) with an examination of how U.S. government (USG) vetting processes and procedures could be enhanced by application of mobile technologies and platforms. The research team identified key mobile platform and security factors to consider when communicating with and screening candidates within the SSC process. This report also describes relevant private-sector practices on talent acquisition, applicant tracking systems (ATSs), screening methods, and communication strategies with candidates prior to the onboarding process.[3] The researchers sought to perform the following tasks for the PAC PMO: (1) categorize emerging mobile technology platforms according to SSC process relevance and ability to assist government vetting of personnel; (2) illustrate relevant practices and lessons learned for integrating security applications with mobile platforms; and (3) provide recommendations on how best to incorporate potentially useful private-sector screening practices to create efficiency within initial stages of the SSC process.

Observations and Suggestions

The findings from each phase of this research are summarized in Table S.1. A more-detailed explanation of our observations and suggestions is presented in Chapter 5 of this report.

Our observations and suggestions for the USG SSC stakeholder community result from the information gained through our public- and private-sector literature review, our interviews with USG vetting stakeholders, and our discussions with the private-sector and mobile technology vendors.[4] Our suggestions also reflect the output of our subject-matter expert (SME) workshop held in April 2022. The observations and suggestions provided in Table S.1 (and in Chapter 5) are not prioritized, since many of the recommended options or actions would likely occur simultaneously across the USG. However, we would suggest further alignment of our proposed recommendations with the Federal Personnel Vetting Guidelines, which could reinforce (and validate) the prioritized initiatives contained therein.[5]

---

[3] The Society for Human Resource Management defines ATSs as a "core platform that collects and stores candidate resumes as well as automates job postings and other manual tasks common to the recruiting function." For more, see Dave Zielinski, "How to Purchase an Applicant Tracking System," Society for Human Resource Management, April 12, 2021.

[4] We use the term *suggestions* to signify options and/or actions that our exploratory research identified as potential benefits for USG SSC stakeholders as they seek to integrate future mobile technology within personnel vetting processes.

[5] A recent Personnel Vetting Reform Quarterly Progress Update notes that the guidelines "describe the vision for creating a personnel vetting program that ensures Americans can trust the Federal workforce to

TABLE S.1

Mobile Technology Research Observations and Suggestions

Observations	Suggestions
Observation 1: The USG has not integrated mobile technology with SSC vetting processes.	• Define and codify mobile vetting policy and guidance. • Conduct legal review of policies and procedures within existing SSC guidance and policy to better understand what is in the realm of the possible. • Capture department and agency practices and lessons learned over the course of the pandemic to ensure that institutional knowledge of virtual vetting is not lost. • Formalize virtual training for investigators and adjudication staff. • Develop strategic messaging to set foundation for vetting culture shift.
Observation 2: Expanding the use of mobile technologies beyond traditional vetting models could uncover additional information sources and shorten investigation timelines.	• Develop scenarios, use cases, and pilots to help identify and align specific technologies to data required in the pre-hire stage. • Ensure that outdated vetting mechanisms do not transition to the mobile environment.
Observation 3: There are opportunities for the USG to adopt several private-sector hiring practices that may improve overall candidate vetting experience.	• Consult with federal organizations actively using ATSs in the hiring process to explore and identify areas that may benefit the SSC process.
Observation 4: Adopting mobile technology could promote a more diverse workforce in accordance with Executive Order 14035[a] and consistent with related priorities for Trusted Workforce (TW) 2.0 implementation.	• Identify areas within the existing application and vetting process that exclude underrepresented candidate populations. • Ensure that a move to mobile does not exclude potential candidates who may not have access to mobile technology.
Observation 5: Identifying metrics for success within a virtual or hybrid working environment could help to ensure that the USG is vetting for the most relevant factors.	• Identify existing questions or categories of position-based screening that may not be as relevant for certain populations of the emerging hybrid or fully remote workforce. • Develop metrics (measures of performance and measures of effectiveness) for determining hybrid and remote work performance goals.
Observation 6: Several hiring flexibilities afforded to USG departments and agencies have proven beneficial during the COVID-19 pandemic but are due to sunset in fiscal year 2023.	• Survey investigators across the SSC enterprise to identify key "pain-points" during the coronavirus disease 2019 (COVID-19) pandemic and determine what specific technologies or processes helped achieve investigative missions during the early stages. • Catalogue informal guidance developed by individual departments and agencies to identify cross-cutting challenges and enablers that could be rapidly operationalized to address hiring and screening in the event of a future global pandemic.

[a] Joseph R. Biden, Jr., Executive Order 14035 "Executive Order on Diversity, Equity, Inclusion, and Accessibility in the Federal Workforce," June 25, 2021.

protect people, property, information, and mission; and moreover, is aligned with and supportive of the Federal government's broader efforts to recruit and retain a diverse and talented workforce." Further, that the "issuance of these Guidelines represents a critical milestone on the path toward full realization of the

Pandemic operating conditions have dictated the need for continued modernization of SSC processes into the mobile realm. COVID-19 conditions demonstrated the USG's national security resilience in maintaining an effective workforce but also revealed a wide range of vulnerabilities across traditional in-person SSC vetting processes. Our discussions with SMEs highlighted that many organizations are reluctant to rely on artificial intelligence (AI), machine learning (ML), or other algorithm-based platforms for vetting despite prolific use of video interviews and other virtual platforms during the pandemic to assist USG candidate screening efforts.[6] This research suggests that mobile technology can enhance—and even replace—some outdated elements of the SSC process in line with TW 2.0 goals and objectives.

Mobile technology offers several advantages over conventional screening processes. Mobile platforms can increase interaction with candidates within the SSC process and with those who may be interested in pursuing a future career in national security. USG-approved mobile platforms may reduce investigator travel needs and other associated administrivia to lessen investigator caseload. Mobile technology could also improve government retention practices; data provided during mobile screening (e.g., skills and interests) in the pre-hire stage could be used to identify additional organizational alignment with career interests (e.g., future jobs, training) that can be outlined and presented to candidates during subsequent onboarding phases.

However, our research shows that even the most "high-tech" mobile device or application will likely not be able to replace the human element. Investigators and adjudicators bring a wealth of empirical experience that is difficult to replicate via software. Detecting anomalies within baseline data is useful for binary data collection, but mobile platforms cannot account for qualitative aspects of human experience required to assess whether an employee should have access to sensitive information.[7]

Finally, this research suggests that availability of technology is not the issue but rather that the institutional vetting culture may present the largest obstacle to future mobile implementation. As our interviews revealed, it is not a matter of *if* a future pandemic or other global event affects the SSC process, but *when*. An institutionalized mobile or virtual process that

---

TW 2.0 personnel vetting model" ("Personnel Vetting Reform Quarterly Progress Update FY 2022, Quarter 1," briefing slides, Performance.gov, 2022; Office of the Director of National Intelligence and the Office of Personnel Management, "Federal Personnel Vetting Guidelines," February 10, 2022).

[6] Our interviews with public- and private-sector stakeholders are governed by Human Subjects Protection Committee (HSPC) protections. The HSPC serves as RAND's Institutional Review Board (IRB) to review and ensure ethical treatment of individuals who are participants in RAND projects through observation, intervention, interaction or use of data about them. RAND's HSPC determined that this research did not constitute human subjects research per the Common Rule, 45 CFR 46. For more, see U.S. Code of Regulations, Title 45, Subtitle A, Subchapter A, Part 46, "Public Welfare."

[7] That is, ML and AI cannot fully assess the *whole person* concept for evaluation of risk, as articulated in investigative or adjudicative guidelines. However, mobile platforms could provide a set of indicators that would be further explored by human staff.

helps to ensure a continuous flow of USG employees could act as a primary safeguard, given our global state of uncertainty.

Contents

APPENDIX

Figures and Tables

Figures

Tables

CHAPTER 1

Introduction

The federal government's traditional in-person and paper-driven methods of managing the security, suitability, and credentialing (SSC) business process can be time-consuming and, in some cases, have caused delays within the vetting process. The U.S. government (USG) has been exploring a variety of technical solutions to expedite, automate, and improve the SSC process as part of the overall Trusted Workforce (TW) 2.0 initiative.[1] TW efforts are aimed at reforming the entirety of the personnel security clearance process to "establish a single vetting system for the U.S. Government."[2] The USG launched the TW Initiative as an iterative process beginning in 2018, following increased congressional scrutiny of overall SSC hiring timelines. TW end-states include the transition of periodic reinvestigations (PRs) for clearance holders to a continuous vetting (CV) model that will increasingly rely on use of technology and supporting infrastructure to support objectives. Figure 1.1 highlights overall timelines and key events within the current TW phased implementation plan.

The Performance Accountability Council (PAC) Program Management Office (PMO) asked the RAND Corporation to explore the possibility (and utility) of incorporating existing or emerging mobile technologies and applications that might facilitate vetting processes in the pre-onboarding phase.[3] The impetus for mobile screening integration has become more urgent within the context of the coronavirus disease 2019 (COVID-19) pandemic; virtual operating conditions have necessitated numerous changes in the way the USG conducts its initial SSC lines of effort.

---

[1] The Office of the Director of National Intelligence (ODNI) announced the TW 2.0 initiative in March 2018 as a means to "identify and establish a new set of policy standards that will transform the U.S. government's approach to vetting its workforce, overhaul the enterprise business processes, and modernize information technology" (Brian Dunbar, "Statement for the Record for Brian Dunbar, Assistant Director, Special Security Directorate, National Counterintelligence and Security Center," testimony before the Senate Select Committee on Intelligence Hearing on Security Clearance Reform, March 7, 2018).

[2] Defense Counterintelligence and Security Agency (DCSA), "Trusted Workforce 2.0 and Continuous Vetting," undated.

[3] Executive Order (EO) 13467 established the SSC PAC to assist in "driving government-wide implementation of security, suitability, and credentialing reform" (George W. Bush, Executive Order 13467, "Reforming Processes Related to Suitability for Government Employment, Fitness for Contractor Employees, and Eligibility for Access to Classified National Security Information," June 30, 2008; SSC PAC PMO, "PAC PMO and Research and Innovation Program Overview," January 2020.

FIGURE 1.1
Trusted Workforce 2.0 Objectives and Implementation Plan

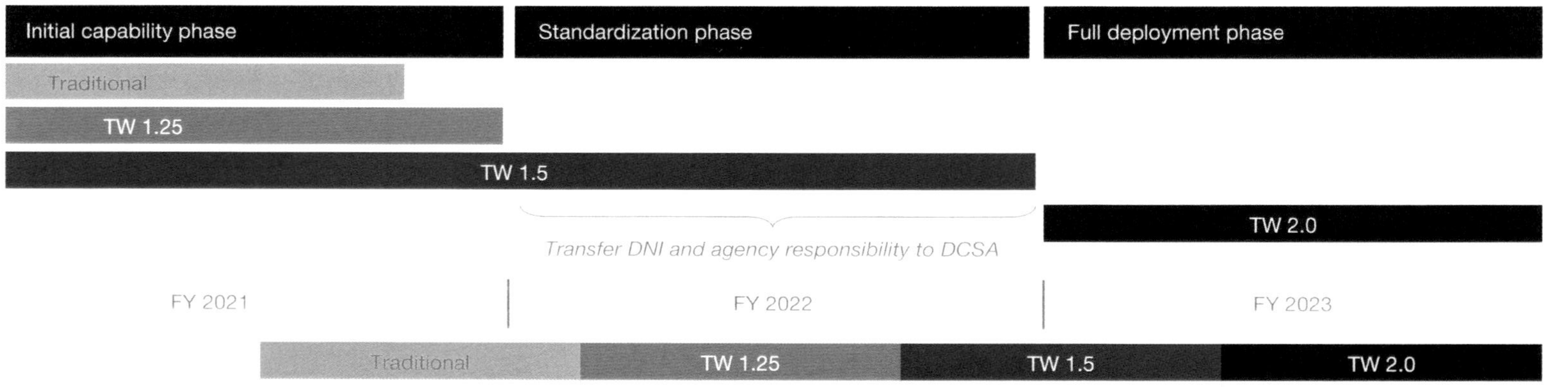

	Traditional (FY 2021)	TW 1.25 (FY 2022)	TW 1.5	TW 2.0 (FY 2023)
Phase	Initial capability phase	Standardization phase		Full deployment phase
Population	Entire federal workforce	National security workforce	National security workforce	Entire federal workforce
Investigative sources	No automated checks	Initial high-value automated checks (3)	Expanded automated checks (7)	Maximum automated checks
CV	Reinvestigations every 5 years	Defers required reinvestigation	Satisfies required reinvestigation	Replaces required reinvestigation
Previously vetted workforce	Full process after two years	Full process after two years	Full process after two years	Minimum process to establish trust
Workforce mobility	Effective for limited % of workforce	Effective for limited % of workforce	Effective for limited % of workforce	Effective for majority of workforce
Integrated IT capability	None	Partially implemented	Moderately implemented	Fully implemented

Transfer DNI and agency responsibility to DCSA

SOURCE: Reproduced from DCSA, undated-b.
NOTE: FY = fiscal year; IT = information technology.

Traditional in-person and paper-based methods of individual pre-hire screening have increasingly shifted to the virtual realm over the past 24 months. In-person interviews with candidates, coworkers, and employers were performed via online video interviews. Various measures to validate candidate identity (e.g., fingerprinting, digital signatures) have been afforded unparalleled flexibilities by several agencies to ensure continuity in the security hiring process. However, many of the processes and procedures developed to address COVID-19–imposed challenges are temporary, and gaps remain in understanding how the existing and transforming SSC process could be improved by integrating mobile technology.

We define mobile technology in line with a recent RAND report that examined mobile data collection and user privacy during the pandemic. For the purposes of this report, mobile technology categories include phone data (e.g., video, voice), platforms, programs, applications, and other virtual abilities that are able to generate "location data generated by GPS (Global Positioning System), Wi-Fi connections, Bluetooth beaconing, or cell towers," including "proximity-based contact or colocation data generated by Bluetooth beaconing or audio signals" and "other personal behavioral data about individuals" that could be "collected by sensors and mobile apps."[4]

Many organizations in the private sector have adopted unique methods and technologies to communicate with and screen candidates during initial hiring stages that may be relevant for the USG to consider as it seeks to meet TW 2.0 milestones. For example, our interviews across the finance, technology, and energy industries highlighted that the use of mobile platforms during candidate hiring phases serve as a preliminary security screening method and help to ensure cultural fit. Nontraditional platforms may be especially important within the COVID-19 context, in which disruptions to traditional personnel vetting (PV) processes can have unforeseen future national security consequences.

This exploratory research report is intended to establish a baseline (factors and considerations) to assist with mobile technology integration into the SSC process. Although mobile technology likely can play a role across other cleared-employee communities (for CV and retention purposes), this research primarily focuses on the application of mobile technology during pre-onboarding phases.

Objectives and Approach

Our research pursued three lines of effort to assist USG thinking about how best to integrate mobile technology into the SSC vetting process. Our first objective was to understand the baseline for use of mobile technology across U.S. departments and agencies during the pre-hire phase. Our second objective was to identify relevant private-sector hiring practices that

---

[4]   Benjamin Boudreaux, Matthew A. DeNardo, Sarah W. Denton, Ricardo Sanchez, Katie Feistel, and Hardika Dayalani, *Data Privacy During Pandemics: A Scorecard Approach for Evaluating the Privacy Implications of COVID-19 Mobile Phone Surveillance Programs*, RAND Corporation, RR-A365-1, 2020.

integrate mobile or other virtual technologies that have the potential to improve overall SSC hiring timelines and improve candidate experience in the SSC process. Our third objective was to synthesize the information from the first two objectives to develop observations and suggestions for how the USG might operationalize mobile technology to support future PV processes under the TW 2.0 initiative.

Researchers on this project used a mixed-methods approach to achieve our research objectives. Our first task included a literature review focused on existing USG mobile and virtual vetting policy, relevant congressional and legal authorities, external USG reviews of the SSC process (e.g., U.S. Government Accountability Office [GAO] and Congressional Research Service [CRS]) and an open-source review (e.g., academic articles and journals). Our literature review also included an examination of relevant hiring practices within the private sector set against the context of the pandemic environment (e.g., the Society for Human Resource Management, Partnership for Public Service).

Our second task sought to obtain information about the hiring process from SSC government stakeholders, private-sector subject-matter experts (SMEs), and mobile technology vendors who provide hiring and screening platforms to USG departments and agencies. The second task helped us to better understand how the USG might leverage mobile platforms to engage and screen prospective government employees. Interviewee feedback was elicited using semi-structured interviews (see Appendix A for a full listing of interviewee questions). The RAND team also conducted an internal workshop with government, human resources (HR), behavioral, and vetting SMEs to further explore interviewee findings and develop possible next steps for USG implementation.

Our final task included synthesizing information gained in the first two tasks toward development of actionable and feasible suggestions for USG vetting stakeholders. These observations and suggestions appear throughout this report and are consolidated and presented in Chapter 5 for readership ease.

Organization of This Report

This report presents our observations, findings, and suggestions to assist future integration of mobile technology into the SSC process. Chapter 2 outlines existing and emerging candidate screening technologies in use by government and private-sector organizations and describes some key challenges and enablers associated with implementation. Chapter 3 summarizes existing USG SSC vetting processes, existing SSC hiring policy and guidance, and some of the hiring flexibilities afforded to USG departments and agencies over the course of the COVID-19 pandemic. In this chapter, we also provide information from our discussions with USG vetting SMEs focused on efforts to incorporate mobile technology into the SSC pre-hiring phase. Chapter 4 presents observations and findings from our discussions with private-sector personnel across a variety of organizations, including our discussions with two mobile technology vendors. Chapter 4 also features a summary of our internal workshop, which is used to support our overall findings, and suggestions for future implementation are presented in Chapter 5.

Scope

Our research primarily focused on the SSC pre-onboarding phase (depicted in Figure 1.2), though it does include some information that may be helpful for later phases of the hiring process, including candidate onboarding, and we describe some ways in which mobile technology may assist in retaining existing USG employees. Additionally, in this report we relied on information that is readily available to the public (i.e., open-source), though we do acknowledge that there are relevant internal government documents and guidance that are not publicly available.[5]

FIGURE 1.2

Phases for Determinations for Personnel Security, Suitability, and Credentialing

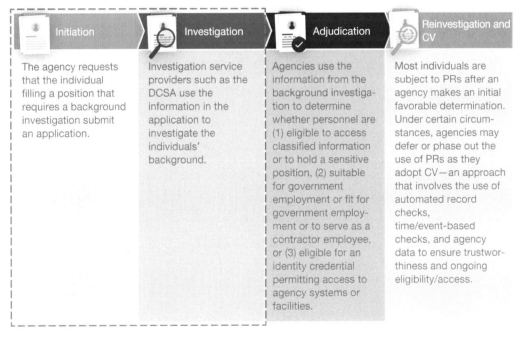

Initiation	Investigation	Adjudication	Reinvestigation and CV
The agency requests that the individual filling a position that requires a background investigation submit an application.	Investigation service providers such as the DCSA use the information in the application to investigate the individuals' background.	Agencies use the information from the background investigation to determine whether personnel are (1) eligible to access classified information or to hold a sensitive position, (2) suitable for government employment or fit for government employment or to serve as a contractor employee, or (3) eligible for an identity credential permitting access to agency systems or facilities.	Most individuals are subject to PRs after an agency makes an initial favorable determination. Under certain circumstances, agencies may defer or phase out the use of PRs as they adopt CV—an approach that involves the use of automated record checks, time/event-based checks, and agency data to ensure trustworthiness and ongoing eligibility/access.

SOURCE: Reproduced from GAO, *Personnel Vetting: Actions Needed to Implement Reforms, Address Challenges, and Improve Planning*, GAO-22-104093, December 2021.

---

[5] Our team considered these sources during the drafting of this report.

CHAPTER 2

The State of Mobile Screening Technology

Overview

This chapter presents our analysis of the public- and private-sector literature focused on the use of mobile screening technologies. We first describe our approach to the literature review, followed by a thematic analysis and categorization of the types of technologies relevant to this study. We conclude this chapter with some overall observations on the state of mobile screening technology, including enablers, challenges, and relevant practices for the USG to consider as it seeks to integrate mobile technology into SSC processes.

Scope and Method

A June 2020 EO highlighted that "modernizing and reforming civil service hiring through improved identification of skills requirements and effective assessments of the skills job seekers possess . . . will provide America a more inclusive and demand-driven labor force."[1] While the scope of this report is primarily focused on the pre-onboarding process, we include some literature examining recruitment, onboarding, and retention to ensure holistic capture of existing uses of technology through the talent management lifecycle. Our key research questions for this task were the following:

1. What key mobile platforms and security factors must be considered when communicating with and screening potential candidates?
2. Are there relevant practices or other lessons learned within the private sector that can help the federal government implement mobile vetting processes successfully?
3. What technological, organizational, legal, and ethical barriers exist to leveraging mobile vetting technologies for hiring federal employees?

We have provided examples of the keywords used to retrieve information in Box 2.1.

---

[1] Donald J. Trump, Executive Order 39457, "Modernizing and Reforming the Assessment and Hiring of Federal Job Candidates," June 26, 2020.

BOX 2.1
Literature Review Search Terms

Organization Types

- Federal agencies
- Private sector (e.g., technology companies, finance, gaming)
- Academia

Keywords

- Mobile vetting
- Cybervetting
- PV
- CV
- Mobile hiring
- Employee monitoring
- Continuous monitoring
- Candidate screening
- Virtual hiring
- Trust
- Candidate experience
- TW
- Human resource management technology
- Skill-based hiring
- Character assessment
- Attitudinal assessment

Over the course of this study, we conducted a review of literature specific to the use of mobile technologies in the workplace. We found that most articles are focused on mobile vetting technologies in the post-onboarding phase (e.g., once an employee is on the job). We also note that the majority of the literature presented below is focused on private-sector organizations; the private sector may appear overly represented in our review, since such practices were established prior to the COVID-19 pandemic.[2] While pandemic operating conditions drove innovation within the federal government to quickly implement and use virtual technologies during hiring and onboarding in a way that had not been accomplished before, such practices are not well represented within the open-source literature. Most of the USG policies that were explored during our review have existed only since February 2020, complicating a more thorough longitudinal analysis of practices deployed. Further, many of the polices analyzed are set to expire in FY 2023, since they were issued as temporary measures in response to COVID-19 pandemic needs.[3]

The following sections present the literature according to relevance to PV and the hiring process. We have also included a more robust annotated bibliography in Appendix C to support observations and findings that appear in this chapter.

---

[2] Information about mobile practices within the private sector, therefore, was more abundant within our open-source searches (both USG investigative managers).

[3] For example, the U.S. Department of Homeland Security (DHS) issued guidance on COVID-19 Form I-9 completion practices on March 20, 2020. While the policy was set to expire on April 30, 2022, DHS has extended the updated flexibilities until October 31, 2022. See DHS, "ICE Announces Extension to I-9 Compliance Flexibility," press release, April 25, 2022a.

Categories of Mobile Technology

The federal government did not aggressively pursue mobile or virtual technologies pre-COVID-19.[4] Since February 2020, policies written to provide mobile and remote flexibilities to USG entities have been limited within the context of a national public health emergency. For example, DHS issued a total of 14 policy updates between March 2020 and April 2022 to provide increased flexibility for determining candidate identity.[5] Initial policies provided employers with the ability to "remotely (e.g., over video link, fax or email, etc.) obtain, inspect, and retain copies of [Employment Eligibility Verification Form I-9] . . . and enter 'COVID-19' as the reason for physical inspection delay."[6] When the national emergency ends, agencies are expected to resume in-person identity vetting procedures.

One week after COVID-19 was declared a global pandemic, the Office of Personnel Management (OPM) released a memorandum stating that federal agencies would be delegated certain hiring authorities, such as waiving the salary offset to reemploy retirees to fill critical positions.[7] Four days later, OPM released guidance to federal agencies on performing onboarding processes remotely "via visual inspection using remote electronic capabilities (e.g., Skype, FaceTime, etc.)"[8]

Figure 2.1 outlines relevant federal government objectives associated with the implementation of mobile technologies across talent management lifecycle phases and includes examples of mobile tools implemented in each phase, as well as key considerations.

Through this literature review, we learned that the use of mobile technology in the hiring process may be beneficial for the federal government, including by reducing the time-to-hire, saving travel costs, and increasing diversity of the federal workforce. While some federal

---

[4]   Some organizations had experimented with video interviews prior to the pandemic.

[5]   For example, see DHS, "ICE Announces Flexibility in Requirements Related to Form I-9 Compliance," press release, March 23, 2020a; DHS, "ICE Announces Extension of Flexibility in Rules Related to Form I-9 Compliance," press release, May 14, 2020b; DHS, "ICE Announces Another 30-Day Extension of Flexibility in Rules Related to Form I-9 Compliance," June 16, 2020c; DHS, "ICE Announces Another Extension to I-9 Compliance Flexibility, No More Extensions for Employers to Respond to NOIs Served in March," press release, July 18, 2020d; DHS, "ICE Announces Another Extension To I-9 Compliance," press release, August 18, 2020e; DHS, "ICE Announces Extension to I-9 Compliance Flexibility," press release, September 14, 2020f; DHS, "ICE Announces Extension to I-9 Compliance Flexibility," November 18, 2020g; DHS, "ICE Announces Extension to I-9 Compliance Flexibility," press release, December 23, 2020h; DHS, "ICE Announces Extension to I-9 Compliance Flexibility," press release, January 27, 2021a; DHS, "ICE Announces Extension, New Employee Guidance to I-9 Compliance Flexibility," press release, March 31, 2021b; DHS, "ICE Announces Extension, New Employee Guidance to I-9 Compliance Flexibility," press release, May 26, 2021c; DHS, "ICE Announces Extension to New Employee Guidance to I-9 Compliance Flexibility," press release, August 31, 2021d; DHS, "ICE Announces Extension to I-9 Compliance Flexibility," press release, December 15, 2021e; and DHS, 2022.

[6]   DHS, 2020a.

[7]   OPM, "Dual Compensation Waiver Requests for COVID-19 Emergency," March 20, 2022.

[8]   OPM, "On-Boarding Processes for New Employees During the COVID-19 Emergency," memorandum, March 24, 2020.

FIGURE 2.1

Categories of Mobile Talent Management Technologies

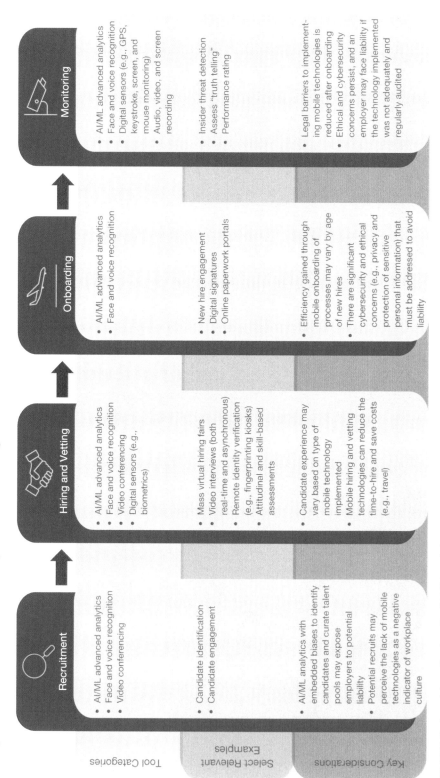

Recruitment

Select Relevant Examples

- AI/ML advanced analytics
- Face and voice recognition
- Video conferencing

- Candidate identification
- Candidate engagement

Key Considerations

- AI/ML analytics with embedded biases to identify candidates and curate talent pools may expose employers to potential liability
- Potential recruits may perceive the lack of mobile technologies as a negative indicator of workplace culture

Hiring and Vetting

- AI/ML advanced analytics
- Face and voice recognition
- Video conferencing
- Digital sensors (e.g., biometrics)

- Mass virtual hiring fairs
- Video interviews (both real-time and asynchronous)
- Remote identity verification (e.g., fingerprinting kiosks)
- Attitudinal and skill-based assessments

- Candidate experience may vary based on type of mobile technology implemented
- Mobile hiring and vetting technologies can reduce the time-to-hire and save costs (e.g., travel)

Onboarding

- AI/ML advanced analytics
- Face and voice recognition

- New hire engagement
- Digital signatures
- Online paperwork portals

- Efficiency gained through mobile onboarding of processes may vary by age of new hires
- There are significant cybersecurity and ethical concerns (e.g., privacy and protection of sensitive personal information) that must be addressed to avoid liability

Monitoring

- AI/ML advanced analytics
- Face and voice recognition
- Digital sensors (e.g., GPS, keystroke, screen, and mouse monitoring)
- Audio, video, and screen recording

- Insider threat detection
- Assess "truth telling"
- Performance rating

- Legal barriers to implementing mobile technologies is reduced after onboarding
- Ethical and cybersecurity concerns persist, and an employer may face liability if the technology implemented was not adequately and regularly audited

Tool Categories

SOURCE: Features information from the RAND team's literature review. See Appendix D for more detail and specific sources.

NOTE: AI/ML = artificial intelligence and/or machine learning.

10

agencies, such as the U.S. General Services Administration (GSA), had begun to develop a digital infrastructure prior to the COVID-19 pandemic, implementation of mobile technologies across the talent management lifecycle appears to have been a direct response to the availability of digital tools and increased hiring authorities after March 2020. Early adopters of hiring technologies—e.g., GSA and the U.S Veterans Health Administration (VHA)—highlighted vulnerabilities within the traditional SSC process that existed before the pandemic.[9] In this report, we focused on *mobile* hiring technologies, as opposed to *remote* hiring technologies—specifically, we focused on technologies, tools, and applications that are compatible with mobile smart phones, tablets, and laptops.[10] The latter includes such examples as fingerprinting kiosks at select U.S. Postal Service (USPS) locations,[11] while the former includes such examples as video conferencing and location data generated by GPS.

Enablers, Challenges, and Relevant Practices

Several enablers, challenges, and practices were presented through the literature.[12] Table 2.1 labels these factors in the Relevance columns according to the following scheme: An *E* signals a description of how mobile technologies have *enabled* hiring practices across organizations. A *C* introduces *challenges* associated with technology implementation. Rows marked *BP* describe some noted mobile technology *best practices* within the literature that are relevant to USG SSC processes.

Summary

This chapter provided a brief overview of our findings from the open-source literature review. As shown in Table 2.1, there are a variety of challenges and enablers associated with technology use in the pre-onboarding stages. Mobile technology enablers include (but are not limited to): reducing time-to-hire, mitigating costs associated with travel (e.g., interviews), and rapid identification of skilled candidate pools. Challenges include a lack of a unified mobile vetting policy, a lack of supporting mobile and digital infrastructure, and the potential for

---

[9]   Jason Miller, "Online Interviews, Virtual Oaths of Office Are Some of the Ways Agencies Are Evolving Hiring," Federal News Network, May 11, 2020; Partnership for Public Service, *Rapid Reinforcements: Strategies for Federal Surge Hiring*, Democracy Fund, October 2020; Heather B. Hayes, "Virtual Tools Allow Agencies to Onboard New Workers from a Distance," *FedTech Magazine*, February 19, 2021; Accenture, "Going Virtual: How Federal Agencies Are Embracing the Hybrid Workforce," *Government Executive*, March 22, 2021.

[10]   This definition of mobile was derived from Boudreaux et al., 2020, p. 4. However, we have revised this definition to include mobile tools that can be used on tablets and laptops.

[11]   Jory Heckman, "USPS Biometrics Program Leans on Its Biggest Asset: A Post Office in Every Neighborhood," Federal News Network, January 12, 2021.

[12]   Some themes emerged as both enablers and challenges. See Appendix C for a more detailed summary of challenges, enablers, and best practices identified during the literature review.

TABLE 2.1

Thematic Analysis of Enablers, Challenges, and Relevant Practices

Theme	Relevance	Description
Time	E	• Mobile hiring technologies can reduce the time-to-hire.
	C	• Typical pre-employment activities (e.g., fingerprinting, physicals, drug testing, reference checks, credentialing) take approximately 30 days. • Federal hiring practices are often insufficient to meet immediate demands for additional talent. • The complexity of the federal hiring process slows it down. • Agencies must balance risk and speed afforded by mobile hiring technologies to ensure the appropriate amount of vetting.
Proliferation	E	• The COVID-19 pandemic accelerated the adoption of mobile technologies used during the hiring process.
Policy	E	• OPM authorized Schedule A hiring authority for federal agencies during the COVID-19 pandemic, which allowed agencies to use excepted service appointments under U.S. Code of Federal Regulations (CFR) Title 5, section 213.3102(i)(3).[a] • OPM authorized federal agencies to perform identity verification inspection virtually. • Within the competitive service, there are noncompetitive hiring authorities that enable agencies to make appointments without using Title 5 competitive examining procedures, thereby streamlining the process and allowing agencies more flexibility when there is a critical need to hire quickly. • OPM's Presidential Management Fellows Program facilitates a process whereby agencies can hire prequalified candidates for a two-year paid position in the excepted service, and agencies may convert fellows to permanent positions in the competitive service.
	C	• There are few permanent (i.e., not temporary) policies to guide implementation of mobile hiring technologies. • There is no national regulation or standard for facial recognition algorithms. • DHS I-9 flexibilities extend only to employers operating entirely remotely. • The federal hiring process hasn't changed in a long time, and there are still regulations in place that dictate the framework by which hiring is conducted. • Details about how the federal hiring process is evolving are difficult to collect. • Options that allow federal agencies to hire qualified staff quickly exist but are not widely known or used (e.g., Schedule A hiring authority). • The typical federal hiring process is less competitive than those in the private sector, as many candidates opt for private-sector position they can secure faster. • Most of the hiring authorities (e.g., Schedule A, Title 38) are limited to the excepted service.
Cost-savings	E	• The use of mobile hiring technologies may reduce the cost of travel (e.g., in-person interview travel).

Table 2.1—Continued

Theme	Relevance	Description
Digital infrastructure	E	• GSA already had much of the digital infrastructure in place at the onset of the COVID-19 pandemic and required only modest adjustments to implement mobile hiring technologies quickly.
	C	• Federal agencies require a robust digital infrastructure to fully leverage mobile hiring technologies (e.g., sorting through thousands of applications from multiple locations at the same time).
Efficiency	E	• Asynchronous video interviews (i.e., interviews not conducted in real time) can eliminate the need for such logistics as scheduling interviews because candidates interview with the automated system at the home on their own timeline. • The VHA reduced the credentialing process from 30 days to 3 days, used data to resolve process inefficiencies, and staggered the onboarding process. • Online assessments can help identify the candidates that align most closely with an agency's needs, competencies, and position requirements.
Ethical, legal, and security implications (ELSI)[b]	C	• Embedded biases in AI/ML tools that lead to inaccuracies may affect hiring decisions, misidentification can make it easier for imposters, and employers can be held liable for use of mobile hiring technologies that have embedded biases that lead to inaccuracies. – Title VII of the Civil Rights Act of 1964[c] – Age Discrimination in Employment Act[d] – Americans with Disabilities Act[e] • Some states are beginning to implement laws that strictly limit how employers use AI/ML to analyze video interviews (e.g., Illinois' Artificial Intelligence Video Interview Act)[f] • Because many mobile hiring technology companies' algorithms are proprietary and not shared publicly, neither candidates nor academics can fully understand how the recorded interviews are evaluated. • Lack of clarity on how sensitive personal information is protected and the cybersecurity robustness of hiring and vetting platforms.
	BP	• Ensure hiring practices—including those beyond the standard federal processes—are transparent and conducive to appropriate oversight. • Employers that deploy mobile hiring technologies have a responsibility to scrutinize the product for bias and discrimination at least as thoroughly as they would look for bugs in software.
Adaptation	C	• Older candidates may struggle to adapt to the virtual hiring environment. • Uptake across the federal government has been slow. • Letting go of traditional hiring practices that aren't reliant on any regulatory requirement has been difficult for some federal agencies.
Candidate experience	C	• Some candidates perceive asynchronous video interviews (i.e., interviews that are pre-recorded) as impersonal and the format as unforgiving.
	BP	• Mandatory preparation for asynchronous video interviews as part of the curriculum at universities. • Agencies need to adopt modern HR approaches that prioritize the candidate and employee experience by building on proven commercial best practices and harnessing the possibilities of new tools and technologies. • Consider candidate choice regarding whether they participate in a video or in-person interview process.

Table 2.1—Continued

Theme	Relevance	Description
Traditional vetting culture	BP	• Physical presence is still considered best practice for identity and employment eligibility verification within the federal government.
Collaboration	BP	• Agency HR directors should work with their respective chief information officers (CIOs) to determine the best ways to implement mobile technologies in their hiring processes. • HR teams should prioritize clear and frequent communication with candidates, as well as with hiring managers, SMEs, agency leaders, and other stakeholders. • Build relationships with IT and other support functions at both the senior and staffing level. • Ensure multiple hiring team members evaluate asynchronous video interviews so the decision on whether a candidate advances in the process is not solely dependent on one person, which can help reduce bias.

Lessons learned	BP	• Federal agencies can learn from GSA and VHA's experience and initial success.
		• There are five critical elements of successful integration of mobile technologies in the hiring process:
		  – predictive validity
		  – transparency and candidate experience
		  – security, privacy, and records retention
		  – candidate pools and efficiency
		  – diversity.
		• Refrain from sacrificing candidate experience for hiring process efficiency.
		• Remove obstacles in the application process to open the aperture to more qualified candidates and put the necessary tools in place so the system is not overwhelmed.
		• Change-management practices are required to implement new mobile technologies and digital tools in the federal hiring process.

SOURCE: RAND literature review and analysis. Please see Appendix C for more detail and specific sources.

NOTE: E = enablers; C = challenges, BP = best or relevant practices.

[a] Code of Federal Regulations, Title 5, Section 213.3102, Entire executive civil service.

[b] While the term ELSI generally refers to ethical, legal, and social implications of applied research, here we have modified the term to refer to ethical, legal, and *security* implications. For more information on the standard use of ELSI, see "What Is ELSI Research?" ELSIhub, undated.

[c] Public Law 88-352, Civil Rights Act of 1964, July 2, 1964.

[d] Public Law 90-202, Age Discrimination in Employment Act of 1967, December 15, 1967.

[e] Public Law 101-336, Americans with Disabilities Act of 1990, July 26, 1990.

[f] Illinois Compiled Statutes, 820 ILCS 42, Artificial Intelligence Video Interview Act, January 1, 2020.

bias within AI/ML platforms. Relevant practices include ensuring transparency and frequent communications during hiring processes, instituting teams of multiple adjudicators to mitigate potential bias, and ensuring integrity (security) of deployed platforms. For readers interested in further exploring the literature used to populate the tables in this chapter, please see Appendix C.

CHAPTER 3

USG Hiring and Screening Processes

Overview

This chapter presents an overview of (1) the USG federal hiring process and the types of job categories that require SSC vetting; (2) the SSC process; and (3) existing USG efforts to incorporate mobile technology into SSC vetting processes. We also provide a brief summary of existing laws, policies, and regulations that would likely govern future implementation of mobile technologies across USG hiring processes.

Overview of USG Federal Hiring Process

The USG federal hiring process can take a variety of forms dependent upon the type of position and the hiring organization. The hiring process may also differ depending on Federal Service Job Categories (e.g., competitive service, excepted service, Senior Executive Service [SES]), permanent or temporary assignments (e.g., internships), or other occupational specialties.[1] This section outlines the federal hiring process at a general level and provides additional references in the footnotes for further reading.

The first stage of the hiring process involves validating hiring needs and requirements against organizational missions and objectives. This may include development of recruitment plans ("to identify the resources and sources for recruitment") and surveying skill gaps across departments and agencies.[2] The second stage includes submission of the Request for

---

[1] U.S. federal job categories are governed through a variety of U.S. Codes (U.S.C.s). The most prominent include United States Code (5 U.S.C. 2102), Parts 213 and 302 of Title 5 of the Code of Federal Regulations, and Title IV of the Civil Service Reform Act (CSRA) of 1978 (Public Law 95-454, Civil Service Reform Act of 1978, October 13, 1978), among others. For more, see OPM, "Policy, Data, Oversight: Hiring Information," undated-c.

[2] Please note that the stages we identify in this section are not a 1:1 match with the "steps" listed on the OPM website. We have abbreviated the steps into stages to provide a brief overview of the hiring processes. For a more thorough listing of hiring steps, please see OPM, "Policy, Data, Oversight: Human Capital Management, Hiring Process Analysis Tool," webpage, undated-d.

Personnel Action (RPA), which provides the hiring managers with the authority required to fill vacant positions.[3] Stages 3 and 4 include organizational review of the job posting requirements (e.g., knowledge, skills, abilities [KSA]) and developing relevant methods for candidate assessment. Assessments may include use of structured interviews, writing samples, or other various written tests.[4] Stages 5, 6, and 7 involve determining position security requirements, posting job announcements, evaluating applications according to the criteria established in stages 3 and 4, and include some initial reference checks prior to interview scheduling. The final stage before a candidate enters on duty may require a security or suitability investigation depending on the type of position-based risk identified by the hiring organization. See Figure 3.1 for a generalized overview of federal hiring stages.

Overview of USG Positions Requiring Background Investigations

This section presents a brief overview of the types of positions and associated risks that factor into position-based security requirements. The level of position-based risk has historically followed the guidelines and tiering structure stipulated within OPM's Position Designation Tool (PDT), although this will soon require updates as the implementation of the TW 2.0 initiative progresses. We have purposefully excluded these specific factors (tiers) from the PDT in Figure 3.1, given the TW 2.0 changes forthcoming—which will collapse the number of investigative tiers from five to three—and the move to a CV model.[5]

The USG generally uses three different forms to initiate candidate background investigations depending on the level of organizational risk posed by an employee serving in specific positions (Box 3.1). The Standard Form (SF) 85 is used to support suitability vetting for candidates who have applied for positions that do not require access to sensitive or classified national security information. The SF-85P is used to support public trust vetting for positions that will require access to sensitive USG information or IT architectures. The SF-86 is used for USG positions requiring access to classified national security information and systems. The SF-86 is used to initiate background investigations for personnel that demonstrate a need to access Confidential information or material (which requires protection), Secret information or material (which requires a substantial degree of protection), or Top Secret information or material (which requires the highest degree of protection).[6]

---

[3] The RPA is outlined in Standard Form-52 (SF-52). For more, see OPM, "Request for Personnel Action," Standard Form 52, Rev. 7/91, U.S. Office of Personnel Management FPM Supp. 296-33, July 1991.

[4] OPM, undated-d.

[5] For more on OPM's PDT, see OPM, "Position Designation Tool," September 2017a.

[6] These designations are sometime annotated as categories of information that may cause "damage" (Confidential), "serious damage," such as disruption of "foreign relations" (Secret), or "exceptionally grave damage," such as the "compromise of vital national defense plans or complex cryptologic and communica-

FIGURE 3.1
Generalized USG Hiring Process

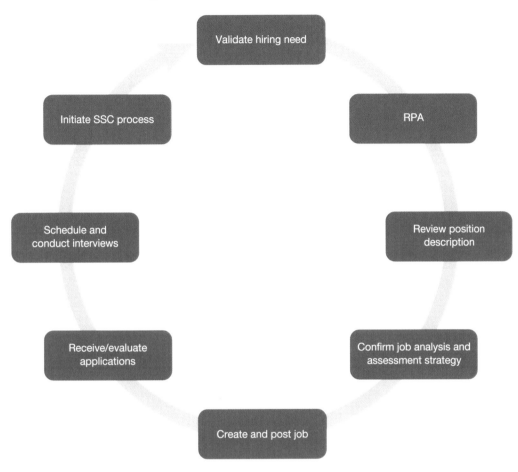

SOURCE: Reproduced from OPM, undated-c.

Suitability and Security Hiring Considerations: The SF-85/SF-86 Population

The suitability and security background investigations share similar end-states (mitigating risk to USG department and agency missions) but are achieved through different levels of vetting mechanisms. U.S. Code of Federal Regulations, Title 5, Section 731.101, Suitability, defines *suitability* as a determination "based on a person's character or conduct that may have an impact on the integrity or efficiency of the service," while a *security clearance* is "an inquiry into an individual's loyalty, character, trustworthiness and reliability to ensure"

---

tions intelligence systems" (Top Secret). See U.S. Code of Federal Regulations, Title 18, Section 3a.11, Classification of Official Information.

BOX 3.1

Federal Investigation Forms and Purpose

SF-85

- Questionnaire for non-sensitive positions
- No work duties requiring access to sensitive or classified national security information
- Example population: Janitorial/housekeeping staff, administrative staff.

SF85-P

- Questionnaire for public-trust positions
- Work duties may require access to sensitive USG information or IT systems
- Example population: Federal law enforcement entities (e.g., Customs and Border Protection [CBP]), federal contract managers.

SF-86

- Questionnaire for national security positions
- Work duties require access to classified or IT systems
- Example population: intelligence analysts, intelligence collectors, program or portfolio managers.

SOURCES: Adapted from OPM, "Forms," webpage, undated-a; and Marko Hakamaa, "Understanding Your Position Designation Determination," Clearance Jobs, November 23, 2013.

continued eligibility for "access to national security information."[7] The type and scope of background investigations and data sources queried for both processes may also vary dependent on organization-specific requirements.[8] Each vetting process may also differ in how investigation results are adjudicated; whereas suitability-based investigations are primarily focused on barring entry to individuals who may cause reputational harm to USG entities (e.g., because of identifiable character traits and conduct), security-based investigations are focused on barring federal employment to individuals who could cause irreparable damage

---

[7]   5 C.F.R. 731.101; ODNI, National Counterintelligence and Security Center, "Security vs Suitability," webpage, undated; also see U.S. Code of Federal Regulations, Title 5, Part 732, National Security Positions; U.S. Code of Federal Regulations, Title 5, Part 1400, Designation of National Security Positions; William J. Clinton, Executive Order 12968, "Access to Classified Information," August 2, 1995; and Bush, 2008.

[8]   TW 2.0 seeks to address inconsistencies in vetting across the USG, including longstanding reciprocity issues between departments and agencies. For more, see GAO, 2021.

to historical, ongoing, or future U.S. national security plans (e.g., because of the risk of classified information leaks).

USG SSC Vetting Process

The USG SSC vetting process is undergoing several reforms through iterations of the TW 2.0 initiative that will likely affect the presentation and explanation of any existing form of PV described in this section.[9] Therefore, in this section, we provide a brief strategic overview of the PV process as it currently exists while noting some of the key elements of TW-reform efforts where relevant.

Sponsoring Organization

Once a candidate has successfully completed initial USG hiring phases (e.g., structured interviews, additional testing, or other assessment methods) and depending on whether the hiring agency allows the temporary onboarding of personnel not yet "cleared," the hiring agency may *sponsor* the candidate for suitability or security screening.[10] The USG organization responsible for the background investigation process varies depending on the sponsoring agency and the arrangements that agency has in place to have the investigation conducted by an authorized investigative agency. For example, U.S. Department of Defense (DoD) candidates for suitability and security vetting have their background investigations conducted by DoD's DCSA.[11] However, DCSA does not conduct investigations for all federal government agencies; other USG organizations, such as the Federal Bureau of Investigations (FBI) and Central Intelligence Agency, serve as their own authorized investigative agencies and conduct their own background investigations for candidates. Agencies that perform their own investigations are designated "Authorized Investigative Agencies," which is an "agency authorized by law, executive order, or designation by the [Security Executive Agent] to conduct a back-

---

[9] For a more thorough explanation of the existing vetting process, see Ryan Andrew Brown, Douglas Yeung, Diana Gehlhaus, and Kathryn O'Connor, *Corporate Knowledge for Government Decisionmakers Insights on Screening, Vetting, and Monitoring Processes*, RR-A275-1, RAND Corporation, 2020.

[10] Some USG departments and agencies may allow the initial onboarding of candidates with long-term employment contingent upon successful adjudication. Other USG entities may instead require candidates to be vetted prior to entering on duty.

[11] Executive Order 13869, issued in April 2019, and additional language in the 2019 National Defense Authorization Act (NDAA) provided additional drivers for transferring the security clearance processing functions from OPM to DCSA. Since FY 2020, responsibility for conducting DoD background checks resides with DCSA. However, DCSA conducts investigations for more than just DoD; according to the DCSA website, "as the primary Investigative Service Provider (ISP) for the Federal Government, DCSA conducts over two million background investigations per year on civilian and military applicants and Federal employees or employees of Government contractors and consultants to Federal programs." For more, see Donald J., Executive Order 13869, "Transferring Responsibility for Background Investigations to the Department of Defense," April 29, 2019; and DCSA, "Background Investigations," webpage, undated-a.

ground investigation of individuals who are proposed for access to classified information or eligibility to hold a sensitive position or to ascertain whether such individuals continue to satisfy the criteria for retaining access to such information or eligibility to hold such positions."[12]

Investigation and Data Collection

Candidates formally enter the background screening process once the designated investigative service provider receives a background investigation request from its sponsoring organization.[13] Initial vetting processes may include contacting in-process candidates to enter information into the online Electronic Questionnaires for Investigations Processing (e-QIP) and signing various forms to allow agencies to perform credit, criminal history, employment, academic, and other checks as determined by vacant position requirements. Investigators may query several different databases to assess criminal, credit, and other historical risk factors depending on the type of investigation.[14] The investigation and data collection phase also includes meetings between investigators and the candidate's family members, work associates, friends, and others listed within relevant sections of SF-85 or SF-86 forms.

Adjudication

All findings from the background investigation phase are transmitted to relevant adjudication officers in the designated authorized adjudicative agency for a final adjudication and determination.[15] A summation of publicly available adjudication guidelines for both the security and the suitability processes are included in Box 3.2. Adjudicators follow the guidelines stipulated within the Security Executive Agency Directive–4 (SEAD-4) for security clearances and 5 C.F.R.

---

[12] ODNI, "Security Executive Agent Directive 6: Continuous Evaluation," January 12, 2018.

[13] A recent RAND report notes that, "The investigation process is conducted by an authorized Investigation Service Provider (ISP); 95 percent of executive branch agencies use the shared service provided by DCSA. Other components of the investigation process—including searches of OPM's Security/Suitability Investigations Index (SII) and the Defense Central Index of Investigations (DCII); review of Federal Bureau of Investigation (FBI) investigation, criminal history, and fingerprint files; and any other agency checks deemed necessary for a position or in relation to the individual's background—are performed by the USG." See Brown et al., 2020.

[14] Examples include the Fingerprint Identification Records System (FIRS), Integrated Automated Fingerprint Identification Systems (IAFIS), Interstate Identification Index (III) National Fingerprint File (NFF), and other databases. For more on use of criminal history record information (CHRI), see RAND Corporation, Federal Bureau of Investigation Criminal Justice Information Services Division, and Bureau of Justice Statistics, *Comparison of Criminal-History Information Systems in the United States and Other Countries*, Bureau of Justice Statistics, April 2, 2020.

[15] Investigative results are adjudicated through Authorized Adjudicative Agencies. Authorized agencies are designated by the Security Executive Agent or delegation by the Suitability Executive Agent (SuitEA). In some situations (e.g., material falsification in a suitability decision), OPM may be uniquely authorized to assume jurisdiction to make government-wide debarment decisions. See ODNI, 2018; Clinton, 1995; and OPM, "Suitability Executive Agent: Suitability Adjudications," webpage, undated-f.

BOX 3.2

Suitability and Security Adjudication Guidelines

SF-85

- Misconduct or negligence in employment
- Criminal or dishonest conduct
- Material, intentional false statement, or deception or fraud in examination or appointment
- Alcohol abuse
- Illegal use of narcotics or other controlled substances
- Engagement in acts or activities designed to overthrow the USG by force
- Any statutory or regulatory bar which prevents the lawful employment.

SF-86

- Allegiance to the United States
- Foreign influence
- Foreign preference
- Sexual behavior
- Personal conduct
- Financial considerations
- Alcohol consumption
- Drug involvement and substance misuse
- Psychological conditions
- Criminal conduct
- Handling protected information
- Outside activities
- Use of IT.

SOURCES: Adapted from U.S. Code of Federal Regulations, Title 5, Section 731.202, Criteria for Making Suitability Determinations; ODNI, 2017.
NOTE: For more on the SF-85P (investigation form used for moderate- and high-risk public trust positions), see OPM, "Questionnaire for Public Trust Positions," December 2017b.

§ 731.202 for suitability determinations to ensure a holistic examination of both positive and negative factors uncovered during the investigation phase.[16] Candidates are then onboarded pending successful completion of the adjudication phase and an affirmative determination.

---

[16] For example, the "nature, extent, and seriousness of the conduct," or the "frequency and recency of the conduct." See ODNI, "Security Executive Agent Directive 4, National Security Adjudicative Guidelines," June 8, 2017.

Periodic Reinvestigation Versus Continuous Vetting

USG employees and contractors who are in positions requiring suitability, public trust, or security clearance undergo PR to reaffirm that they should have continued access to government facilities and/or sensitive or classified information and platforms. The frequency of the PR may vary depending on the type of position and final adjudicated clearance level of the employee but is generally five to ten years. The move to a CV model, once fully implemented via TW 2.0, will replace the requirements for PRs. CV includes automated record checks and requires abilities to ingest real-time alerts (e.g., insider threat systems) into the CV IT architecture.[17]

Summary

Candidates who have completed initial hiring phases are sponsored by their hiring agency for suitability, public trust, or security screening. A gaining agency may also make a preliminary determination to onboard an individual based on preliminary checks, or it may wait for a full adjudicative determination. Investigators will compile candidate-provided information (e.g., SF-85 or 86) and collect other relevant data on an individual's background (including the conduct of interviews for some levels of investigation). This information is then adjudicated according to specific guidelines to provide a final determination to grant access at the appropriate level. Currently, those who are in positions requiring suitability, public trust, or security clearance are reinvestigated every five to ten years; this will soon change to a CV model under the TW 2.0 initiative.

Relevant Privacy and Legal Considerations for Mobile and Virtual Hiring

Several legal, policy, and other organization-specific documents guide USG hiring practices and offer various civil protections to federal employment candidates. In this section, we briefly review the policy and guidance most pertinent to the future mobile technology integration.[18] We have categorized these policy considerations below along three possible uses of mobile technology in the pre-hire phase. This includes candidate monitoring (e.g., facial

---

[17] DCSA notes that the move to CV entails "regularly reviewing a cleared individual's background to ensure they continue to meet security clearance requirements and should continue to hold positions of trust. Automated record checks pull data from criminal, terrorism, and financial databases, as well as public records, at any time during an individual's period of eligibility." For more, see DCSA, "DCSA Enrolls U.S. Security Clearance Holders in Continuous Vetting Program," press release, October 1, 2021; and DCSA, "Trusted Workforce 2.0: The Future of Personnel Vetting," *CDSE Pulse*, Vol. 2, No. 7, July 2021.

[18] OPM hosts a website containing information about USG hiring authorities and flexibilities, candidate assessment techniques, and employment laws and regulations. For a full listing of guidance and policy, see OPM, undated-c.

recognition, AI/ML platform use during interviews), data collection (e.g., identity, biometric markers), and data storage and retrieval. Of note, there is no single U.S. law or policy that would govern the entirety of factors associated with mobile technology implementation. See Box 3.3 for a brief overview of the policies that appear in this section.

Mobile/Virtual Technology Monitoring

Fourth Amendment protections within the U.S. Constitution and the Privacy Act of 1974 serve as the primary mechanisms to safeguard candidates in the pre-hire stage. The "search and seizure" language within the Fourth Amendment would prevent the unauthorized monitoring, collection, or storage of candidate information without explicit consent of the prospective employee.[19] The Administrative Procedure Act (APA) further requires federal departments and agencies to publicly list and describe the use of any technologies, processes, or procedures that a candidate may be subject to during the pre-hire stage.[20] Any future implementation of mobile technology into the initial stages of the SSC process would likely require a public listing of the technology or platform in use within the Federal Register, similar to listings (and the protections) required for use of polygraph examinations.[21] Future mobile or virtual technology vetting integration would also require a crosswalk with CFR Title 5 (i.e., legal authorities for employers, Merit System Protection Board) regulations and principles to protect various protected employee categories.[22]

Mobile/Virtual Technology Data Collection

Several U.S. laws and institutional policies would affect mobile data collection in the pre-hire phase.[23] The Authorization for Release of Information signatory pages found at the end of the SSC forms (e.g., SF-86) allow the USG to collect criminal history, financial, and medical record data as part of the overall investigative process. Use of mobile vetting during the candidate pre-hire phase to generate data would likely require similar authorizations and candidate notifications. 5 U.S.C. 9101 (CHRI), Pub. L. 104–191 (HIPPA), and 15 U.S.C. § 1681 (Fair Credit Reporting Act) have traditionally served as the mechanism to guide USG data collection during investigation phases, though these laws may not be well positioned to address additional privacy concerns within the virtual realm.

---

[19] For more on Fourth Amendment federal cases relevant to mobile screening technology, see Stephanie Jurkowski, "Electronic Surveillance," webpage, Cornell Law School Legal Information Institute, July 2017; and 5 USC § 552a.

[20] Pub. L. 79-404, 1946.

[21] For example, see U.S. Code, Title 29, Chapter 22, Employee Polygraph Protection.

[22] For more on Title 5 regulations, see 5 CFR.

[23] U.S. states may also have additional privacy laws that affect use of mobile technology. See Thorin Klosowski, "The State of Consumer Data Privacy Laws in the US (and Why It Matters)," *New York Times*, September 6, 2021.

BOX 3.3

Relevant Policy and Guidance for Mobile Technology Use

Data Monitoring

- Fourth Amendment[a]
- Privacy Act of 1974[b]
- APA[c]
- CFR Title 5.

Data Collection

- 5 U.S.C. 9101 (CHRI)[d]
- Public Law 104–191 (HIPPA)[e]
- 15 U.S.C. § 1681 (Fair Credit Reporting Act)[f]
- Electronic Communications Privacy Act of 1986 (ECPA), 18 U.S.C. §§ 2510-2523[g]
- SEAD-5.[h]

Data Storage

- 5 U.S.C. § 552a
- [Has crossover with policy listed under monitoring, collection].

Platform/Technology Security

- Federal Information Security Management Act (FISMA)
- Federal Risk and Authorization Management Program (FedRAMP)
- Federal information processing standard (FIPS)
- Defense Information Systems Agency–Security Technical Implementation Guides (DISA-STIG)
- National Institute for Standards and Technology (NIST) SP 800-163.[i]

[a] *Constitution of the United States*, National Archives, 1787, Amendment IV.

[b] Public Law 93–579, Privacy Act of 1974, December 31, 1974.

[c] Public Law 79-404, Administrative Procedure Act, June 11, 1946.

[d] U.S. Code, Title 5, Section 9101, Access to Criminal History Records for National Security and Other Purposes.

[e] Public Law 104-191, Health Insurance Portability and Accountability Act (HIPPA) of 1996, August 21, 1996.

[f] U.S. Code, Title 15, Section 1681, Fair Credit Reporting Act.

[g] U.S. Code, Title 18, Sections 2510–2523, Electronic Communications Privacy Act of 1986.

[h] ODNI, "Security Executive Agent Directive 5: Collection, Use, and Retention of Publicly Available Social Media Information in Personnel Security Background Investigations and Adjudications," May 12, 2016.

[i] NIST, "Vetting the Security of Mobile Applications," SP 800-163, Revision 1, April 19, 2019a.

The ODNI issued SEAD-5 in 2016 to provide investigative agencies with clarifying information and boundaries regarding social media data collection not otherwise found within existing legislation.[24] Future mobile technology integration would also require alignment with the policies outlined within ECPA, 18 U.S.C. §§ 2510–2523.

Mobile/Virtual Technology Data Storage

5 U.S.C. § 552a provides definitions for the types of data that may be transmitted and stored during mobile sessions between investigators and candidates. 5 U.S.C. § 552a is comprehensive; records are defined as "any item, collection, or grouping of information about an individual that is maintained by an agency, including, but not limited to, his education, financial transactions, medical history, and criminal or employment history and that contains his name, or the identifying number, symbol, or other identifying particular assigned to the individual, such as a finger or voice print or a photograph."[25]

5 U.S.C. § 552a also provides authorities for how automated records checks ("matching programs") may be used in the SSC hiring process, such as using candidate-derived data to query counterintelligence databases or to " produce background checks for security clearances of Federal personnel or Federal contractor personnel."[26] USG investigative organizations must also abide by a variety of additional data storage requirements outlined in 5 U.S.C. § 552a. There are three key requirements relevant to mobile vetting: (1) to maintain individual records that are "relevant and necessary"; (2) to collect data "to the greatest extent practicable directly from the subject individual when the information may result in adverse determinations about an individual's rights, benefits, and privileges under Federal programs"; and (3) to "inform each individual whom it asks to supply information, on the form which it uses to collect the information or on a separate form that can be retained by the individual."[27] Future mobile technology implementation would need to ensure that data collection and subsequent storage directly pertains to the SSC process and to ensure transparency in using any mobile platform or technology during interviews or other communications with the candidate.

Mobile/Virtual Technology Security

Future SSC mobile technology integration will need to follow federal policy and guidance governing the security of any deployed platform. FISMA, The Federal Risk and Authorization Management Program (FedRAMP), FIPS, and DISA STIGs provide policy frameworks

---

[24] ODNI, 2016.

[25] 5 U.S.C. § 552a.

[26] 5 U.S.C. § 552a.

[27] 5 U.S.C. § 552a.

for ensuring end-to-end security of USG technology platforms.[28] FISMA outlines protection measures (e.g., cybersecurity) to ensure platform security integrity against U.S. adversaries or other external USG entities. FedRAMP provides guidelines for protection of USG cloud-based IT infrastructure. FIPS lists various IT protection standards for platform encryption and digital signatures.[29] The DISA-STIGs are uniquely focused on safeguarding DoD's suite of IT platforms. However, existing legislation and departmental policies may not adequately account for the types of protection (e.g., encryption) required for mobile technology use within the SSC process.

NIST provides some additional factors for consideration that begin to set the baseline needed to explore mobile technology integration. NIST publication SP 800-163 focuses on various aspects of mobile technology screening, including mobile application security requirements, application testing (for risks and system vulnerabilities), threats to mobile applications (e.g., ransomware, short message service (SMS) fraud), and application scoring systems that may help SSC stakeholders identify what types of characteristics would be required for full implementation.[30]

Summary

Multiple U.S. laws or policies likely govern the range of factors associated with mobile technology implementation. For mobile or virtual monitoring, the Fourth Amendment requires explicit consent for monitoring, while the APA requires monitoring technologies and platforms that the government uses to be publicly listed. For mobile and virtual data collection, additional authorizations and candidate notifications would likely be needed to collect criminal history, financial, or medical information in the pre-hire phase. For mobile and virtual data storage, U.S.C. specifies data that can be transmitted and stored and how they can be used. As an example, such data storage would need to be directly relevant for vetting and transparent to the candidate. For mobile and virtual data security, federal cybersecurity policy and digital infrastructure standards offer guidance on security requirements, integration, and testing.

---

[28] End-to-end processes include from the point of acquisition (e.g., supply chain) though implementation and use.

[29] Among others. See NIST, "Compliance FAQs: Federal Information Processing Standards (FIPS)," webpage, November 15, 2019b.

[30] NIST, 2019a.

Efforts to Incorporate Mobile Technology into USG Hiring Practices

Section Overview

This section presents an overview of our discussions with USG vetting SMEs conducted between January and March 2022. The RAND team spoke with five individuals across four organizations that have responsibilities in developing guidance and policies for SSC vetting. Some of the individuals we spoke with also have investigator management responsibilities and direct knowledge of existing and emerging technologies to support candidate background screening.

Several interviewees drew distinctions between mobile and remote vetting that we had not initially considered. While the USG does not currently deploy any mobile platforms to screen candidates, the USG does use remote (physical) kiosks to assist with gathering candidate fingerprints, paperwork, and signatures. Interviewees reported that several USPS offices across the United States have assisted in the collection of candidate data to facilitate security and suitability screening, including to process USG Common Access Cards for onboarding credentials. GSA has developed a Personal Identity Verification (PIV) program called USAccess that allows agencies to accept kiosk-obtained information from in-process candidates.[31] The USAccess program was established in 2016 by the Office of Management and Budget to "provide PIV credentialing services and support for federal employees and contractors at established locations throughout the country."[32] GSA staff have also provided USPS personnel with relevant training needed to monitor and process PIV-related applicants.[33]

Mobile Technology Enablers

Interviewees reported that conducting investigator-based surveys to identify the "biggest pain-points" in the initial screening process may assist in identifying relevant mobile platforms with characteristics required to support candidate processing. USG interviewees also suggested several other vetting mechanisms that could be enabled through future mobile technology implementation; they are included below.

Rapid Data Acquisition

Mobile applications may assist in the rapid acquisition of court records or other legal documents that might otherwise lead to processing delays. Mobile platforms that could scan, process, and send results to cloud-based servers reportedly would offer significant time savings

---

[31] GSA, "USAccess: Identity, Credentials, and Access Management," webpage, undated.

[32] GSA, undated; also see Shaun Donovan, "Improving Administrative Functions Through Shared Services," Office of Management and Budget, Memorandum M-16-11, May 4, 2016; and Mick Mulvaney, "Comprehensive Plan for Reforming the Federal Government and Reducing the Federal Civilian Workforce," Office of Management and Budget, Memorandum M-17-22, April 12, 2017.

[33] Two USG suitability and credentialing SMEs.

over current methods.[34] Interviewees mentioned that mobile applications could allow investigators to obtain field-based biometrics (e.g., pictures for facial recognition or fingerprints) during interviews, rather than relying on other paper-based tools.

Mobile-based video interviewing (VI) (as opposed to desktop suites) could save time and costs associated with travel and could allow investigators to conduct interviews away from their offices. The expanded use of virtual interviews could also save travel time and costs associated with existing cleared population that are based overseas. Interviewees also noted that mobile technology might be best used prior to submission of the SF-86 (or 85) to pre-populate various fields (e.g., previous addresses, employment history) and post-submission as a means to detect anomalies (e.g., listed one address but lived at another).[35]

Improve Candidate Vetting Experience

Interviewees noted that layering mobile technology with AI programs might assist with pro-actively messaging candidates about missing information, typos, and other errors that can cause delays in e-QIP submissions. Future mobile technology implementation might also enable hiring organizations to conduct "mass-screening" events to create "pre-cleared" pools of candidates who could be proactively messaged (e.g., chats, emails) about upcoming job openings. Creating pre-cleared pools may also signal the types of relevant skills or tools candidates have and can address emerging USG problem sets.[36]

Increase Workforce Diversity

Deploying mobile technology may be especially useful for increasing the diversity of the USG workforce. Existing USG job platforms and the associated visibility of those platforms may not be readily apparent (or accessible) to large portions of the eligible workforce. Our interviewees suggest that mobile technology could act as a force multiplier in helping to advertise to and recruit individuals who traditionally may not be familiar with USG job roles, benefits, or other unique skill development.

Mobile Technology Challenges
No Official Policy or Strategy for Mobile Technology–SSC Integration

TW 2.0 end-states featured prominently in discussions with USG vetting SMEs.[37] Much of the current planning in the organizations we spoke with is focused on aligning IT resources

---

[34] USG investigative manager.

[35] "We aren't just trying to keep bad people out the government, we are also trying to clear good people in a reasonable amount of time . . . trying to find something that we can bake in that gets the information to the investigator so they aren't spinning their wheels would be great" (USG investigative manager).

[36] One agency has tailored its job postings to positions, rather than locations, to generate a more diverse pool of applicants. This agency also offers several locations for structured interviews, choice of polygraph location, and other job-relevant requirements intended to provide candidates flexibility (two USG suitability and credentialing SMEs).

[37] For more, see DCSA, undated-b.

to support CV, which will replace traditional PR across federal departments and agencies. While the agencies we spoke with confirmed that internal planning processes and procedures are being developed to align existing vetting systems with priorities identified within TW 2.0 initiatives, interviewees noted that no existing policies or strategies have yet aligned specific technologies to pre-onboarding stages.[38] One USG vetting SME noted that the use of mobile technology to enable vetting is not on the horizon or part of any existing planning discussions.[39] Another noted that "We would be naïve to think the future will not have this be part of the security clearance process."[40]

One vetting program manager noted that "lots" of internal executive memos began to appear as the pandemic started to surge in early 2020.[41] The program manager highlighted that approvals for video interviews provided some flexibility to continue vetting operations without the need for in-person contact. DoD began conducting some VI pilots prior to the COVID-19 pandemic via the Commercial Virtual Remote (CVR) Program, which included Microsoft Teams.[42] Interviewees suggested that the early-pilot success of the CVR platform likely enabled USG vetting activities to continue once the pandemic expanded.[43]

Some government SMEs with investigative responsibilities expressed concerns related to the security of deployed mobile platforms. Candidates typically do not have access to USG-approved devices, which may be problematic for processing and transmitting candidate personally identifiable information (PII) between devices. The USG investigative managers also alluded to the possibility of an adversarial breach of mobile data or devices that could be used to access or disrupt SSC-wide systems and process, though they noted that there are a variety of desktop applications that "could" transition into a mobile environment in the future if appropriate digital safeguards were in place.[44]

---

[38] Both USG investigative managers, F, and two USG suitability and credentialing SMEs. Subsequent discussion with USG personnel noted that the USG is funding a preliminary effort to explore the use of an "eInterview" mobile application, which will collect information from individuals using eInterview question sets. The eInterview is envisioned to be a computer-assisted self-interview in which respondents either read or listen to questions delivered by a computer program.

[39] USG investigative manager.

[40] USG investigative manager.

[41] USG investigative manager.

[42] Jared Serbu, "Adieu to CVR, the Platform That Taught DoD How to Act as an IT Enterprise," Federal News Network Radio, June 21, 2021.

[43] One interviewee noted that, "we had to scale that quickly with COVID from both our side and the end user perspective . . . couldn't go to a place of business and talk to people because they weren't there so the option for in-person wasn't there even if it was the preferred method. . . . We had the ability to use VI and we quickly looked at the platforms we had available like CVR (MS Teams) and we trained our staff in a lot of virtual online training and went pretty quickly from pilot to full implementation" (USG investigative manager).

[44] Both USG investigative managers we interviewed described a scenario similar to the 2015 OPM data breach. For more, see GAO, *Information Security: OPM Has Improved Controls, but Further Efforts Are*

Not All Hiring Flexibilities Afforded During the Pandemic Will Continue

Discussions with vetting personnel highlighted some hiring flexibilities that were extended in the wake of the pandemic, though they expressed concern over their temporal nature. Some USG departments and agencies have developed organization-unique (informal) guidance for virtual hiring over the past 18 months.[45] For example, DHS's Immigration and Customs Enforcement (ICE) has USG-wide screening responsibilities to confirm U.S. citizenship for security and suitability determinations through the I-9 Employment Eligibility Verification form.[46] Hiring flexibilities during the pandemic included the deferment of "physical presence requirements" that traditionally have been used to establish candidate identity. DHS physical-presence deferment guidance notes that, "Employers with employees taking physical proximity precautions due to COVID-19 will not be required to review the employee's identity and employment authorization documents in the employee's physical presence."[47] However, such I-9 hiring flexibilities were due to sunset in October 2022.[48]

Other USG departments and agencies have issued similar guidance intended to help organizations understand available screening and hiring flexibilities within the same period.[49] OPM maintains several websites that include COVID-19–related hiring and onboarding flexibilities for USG reference. One OPM memo directs agencies to defer fingerprint requirements for candidates (or employers) who are unable to proceed with in-person processing.[50] Other posted guidance directs USG organizations to proceed with virtual Oaths of Office during the federal onboarding process to prevent processing delays.[51] OPM also provides several toolkits designed to help USG organizations understand how certain populations of the federal workforce can transition to remote or hybrid work.[52]

NIST has also released guidance to support the development of remote hiring technologies. The NIST-published FIPS 201 provides guidance and requirements for virtual identity

---

Needed, GAO-17-614, August 3, 2017.

[45] Two USG suitability and credentialing SMEs.

[46] DHS, "I-9, Employment Eligibility Verification," November 10, 2022b.

[47] For a full listing of temporary I-9 policies related to COVID-19, see U.S. Citizenship and Immigration Services, "Temporary Policies Related to COVID-19," webpage, July 22, 2022b.

[48] U.S. Citizenship and Immigration Services, "DHS Extends Form I-9 Requirement Flexibility," press release, April 25, 2022a.

[49] One interviewee reported that the USG has conducted pilot programs with seven USPS facilities to explore options for remote fingerprinting.

[50] One hiring agency reported that it had adopted OPM guidance and developed its own procedures for obtaining virtual signatures for documents in an attempt to generate a "Turbo-Tax" type of form for candidates (two USG suitability and credentialing SMEs). Also see Michael J. Rigas, "Temporary Procedures for Personnel Vetting and Appointment of New Employees During Maximum Telework Period Due to Coronavirus COVID-19," memorandum, Office of Personnel Management, March 25, 2020.

[51] OPM, 2020.

[52] For example, see OPM, "Hybrid Work Environment Toolkit," toolkit, undated-b.

verification to receive USG-issued PIV credentials.[53] NIST also released (prepandemic) guidance for vetting mobile technology platforms, which may be helpful as the USG seeks to integrate mobile platforms into pre-hire screening.[54]

Working in the Virtual or Hybrid Environment Poses New Risks to USG Organizations

USG vetting organizations typically categorize risk in two ways: risk-in-person (e.g., criminal history, chemical dependency), and risk-in-position (e.g., access to sensitive information or materiel). Working within a hybrid office model may present new or amplify existing risk factors when planning for mobile vetting implementation. Most of our interviewee comments were directed at USG personnel in existing government positions but suggested that such factors could extend to candidates in the pre-hire stage.

Working in a remote environment decreases peer and manager observation of individual behaviors and actions that are otherwise readily observable in an office environment.[55] "Water-cooler" chats, hallway discussions, and other informal methods of communication can provide unique risk-in-person indicators that may be difficult to replicate in a virtual environment.[56] Financial strain, boredom, substance abuse, or other mental health issues related to isolation may be empirically impossible to detect without CV data collection.[57] Interviewees suggest that any mobile technology deployed to assist vetting in the pre-hire stage will need to account for or acknowledge possible personality-trait gaps that are unobservable during remote interviewing.

The proximity of family members, friends, roommates, or other cohabitants to employees and their USG devices (e.g., phones, laptops) may increase the prevalence of position-based risk. Conferences, meetings, emails, and other on-screen documents once only found within the in-office environment may now be within earshot or viewing distance of individuals who are not affiliated with USG organizations. While current screening methods ask candidates to provide information about co-habitants, such questions are likely aimed at understanding

---

[53] NIST, "Personal Identity Verification (PIV) of Federal Employees and Contractors," FIPS 201-3, January 2022.

[54] NIST, 2019a.

[55] One suitability SME noted that decreased interaction with existing coworkers makes it difficult to establish baseline employment history, especially for individuals who have transitioned to new jobs during the pandemic.

[56] One interviewee noted, "What I'm more worried about is the human intel side of the house. . . . for us you have to list friends and neighbors or people you've had contact with over the span of the investigation; we make sure it's someone you socialize with in-person. . . . now what do those contacts look like when people for the most part haven't been meeting in-person? Anybody who during COVID had the propensity for going rogue and didn't have contact with anyone, that's a bigger worry than third-party access" (USG investigative manager).

[57] And even then, such information may not be reported or recorded.

the character of the candidate in-process rather than the types of risk those cohabitants pose to a candidate who may be working remotely.[58]

The proliferation of hybrid work environments presents additional adversary access points via USG-affiliated devices. Employees working from home may not always use USG virtual private networks to establish trusted connections or may conduct a variety of personal tasks (e.g., banking, shopping) on USG devices that could expose USG IT systems to increased external risk. Interviewees suggested that the characteristics of mobile technology to screen applicants should consider how best to identify habits or behaviors that could pose additional risks within remote-work environments.

Ability to Integrate Mobile Technology into the Pre-Hiring Process Faces Numerous Legal Challenges

Our vetting SMEs highlighted that existing legal and policy implications could limit overall implementation of mobile technology in the pre-hire stage. Fourth Amendment constitutional protections, e-Government Act (18 U.S.C. 119), Privacy Act, and FISMA authorities dictate several requirements that would likely factor into any implementation of digital screening. Freedom of Information Act laws also prevent the recording or storage of candidate video-interviews. These SMEs suggested that any future integration of mobile technology would require authorizations similar to candidate polygraph consent forms and would require public listing within the APA.[59] SMEs suggested that the use of an extended probationary period might be useful, since the USG may deploy additional mobile-screening mechanisms once candidates are onboarded.

Unclear Returns on Investment During the COVID-19 Pandemic

Much of the value derived from the use of VI, both before and during the pandemic, is anecdotal.[60] Our interviews highlighted that, while process efficiency and investigator caseload were enabled through the use of video interviews, it was unclear whether any departments or agencies have conducted any type of cost-per-hire assessment of traditional processes versus mobile processes.[61] One USG SME noted that DCSA has a department focused on "data-driven analytics" that may be able to serve as a research baseline for efficiencies gained

---

[58] Both USG investigative managers and suitability and credentialing SMEs.

[59] The APA is a federal law that directs the administrative functions of executive branch agencies. The APA stipulates that all agencies must publish their regulations in the Federal Register to provide the public with notice (and room for comment) before regulations are implemented.

[60] However, the research team notes the increased timeliness of SSC adjudications within recent TW 2.0 documentation that may help to serve as a baseline.

[61] One SME with investigative experience offered this vignette: "[In] Alaska, for example, an investigator might have to cover part of the state, and they would have to fly from community to community prepandemic and that's a challenge . . . as we define what's in-person and what we can do with a video interview, then they can say 'these five or six things can be done by video' because there's no other issues on the case, we would naturally have timeliness and efficiency gains; we are going to see major gains there from an investigative, cost, and time standpoint" (USG investigative manager).

during use of video interviews and follow-up questioning of candidate-listed contacts.[62] One federal law-enforcement organization we spoke with also reported use of an automated tool to assist with candidate interview scheduling and interviews, which reportedly offered an annual cost-benefit of $2 million.[63]

Training (People and Platforms)

Our interviews with USG investigative program managers highlighted that there is limited video interview (or other virtual or mobile technology) training available to vetting staff. Interviewees suggested that candidate mannerisms and other behavior indicators during traditional in-person interviews may not be readily observable in a virtual setting.[64] During the COVID-19 pandemic, investigative agencies provided some limited VI training to those conducting video interviews, though they retained the authority to conduct follow-up in-person interviews if a candidate relayed information or behaviors that indicated increased risk (e.g., domestic violence or other criminal acts).[65] Another key challenge includes training investigators for virtual administrative functions, including scheduling (generating reliable links for connections with interviewees), "dealing with" bandwidth issues, and alternative methods for contact in the event of disconnection.[66]

Interviews with USG vetting staff also covered training within the context of future AI/ML screening implementation. Staff expressed concerns about "training" mobile platforms to be able to detect anomalies within data provided by candidates during the pre-hire stage.[67] Most felt that, while some processes could be automated through mobile platforms, others would need to retain a human in the loop to ensure established vetting standards and mitigate potential risks from an overreliance on technology.

Vetting for Skills

Some USG organizations have contracts with private-sector technology companies to assist with screening candidates for skill-based competencies. However, USG vetting agencies are

---

[62] One of the two USG investigative managers we interviewed reported that piloting an "in-motion" study for investigators may be useful for understanding time spent on travel versus efficiencies gained during virtual questioning.

[63] USA Staffing and USAJobs also reportedly use automation software to determine whether individuals have registered for Selective Service without the candidate needing to manually enter information (two USG suitability and credentialing SMEs).

[64] For example, foot tapping or fidgeting. However, our interviews suggested that VI is preferable to phone conversations, which provide even fewer indicators.

[65] USG investigative manager.

[66] Both USG investigative managers.

[67] One interviewee commented that, "that's my biggest fear with AI, that there's variables that there's no one set of questions the investigator asks; don't know how you can build an AI that could do that. . . . maybe you can and I don't know. . . . that's my biggest fear. . . . I'm not antitechnology or against trying to figure out the art of the possible but think we have to be careful of application and do get worried that we'd be missing a lot of key things unless it's done correctly" (USG investigative manager).

primarily focused on creating investigative "packages" that indicate areas of possible risk for adjudication, while the requesting organization (or clearance sponsor) is responsible for assessing and validating candidate skills or other KSAs.[68] Two USG interviewees who are suitability and credentialing SMEs suggested that online screening from such as the e-QIP could accommodate the incorporation of skill-screening technologies that could add value during the interview process.[69] The same interviewees highlighted that, although there is a disbarment process for candidates who have "inflated" academic credentials or skill-based certifications, the current automated process can struggle to tie disparate pieces of information together for investigators.[70]

Virtual Adjudication

As mentioned earlier in this chapter, investigative results are adjudicated by an authorized adjudicative agency; for example, in DoD's case, they are transmitted to DoD's Consolidated Adjudication Services (CAS) for final adjudication and determination. Security and Suitability investigation results are adjudicated through Authorized Adjudicative Agencies. Authorized agencies are designated by the Security Executive Agent or delegation by the SuitEA. In some situations (e.g., material falsification in a suitability decision), OPM may be uniquely authorized to assume jurisdiction to make government-wide debarment decisions.[71] One USG interviewee with investigative subject-matter expertise with whom we spoke was unclear whether there were different adjudicative mechanisms for interviews or investigations that were conducted within a virtual environment. One vetting agency noted that VI-based interview results used the same Federal Investigative Standards as in-person interviews, while others were unable to provide additional information; however, interviewees with investigative experience suggested that the identification of additional virtual-interview metrics may be required if the use of VI continues in a post–COVID-19 environment.[72]

---

[68] USG investigative manager, two USG Suitability and Credentialing SMEs, and a senior USG talent acquisition program manager for a federal law enforcement organization.

[69] For example, if a candidate lists particular skills (e.g., data scientist) but is not able to complete a basic online assessment of coding capabilities (two USG suitability and credentialing SMEs).

[70] Verification appears entirely dependent on clearance-sponsor capabilities (two USG suitability and credentialing SMEs).

[71] See ODNI, 2018; Clinton, 1995; and OPM, undated-f.

[72] One interviewee noted, "that needs to be explored to see. . . . The hypothesis would be in theory that if we do a VI or in-person, ideally our hypothesis is that we will get the same answer, but that needs to be looked at particularly in how much information we have developed . . . average amount of issues higher or lower versus video or in-person, could be that they tell us more in VI because they are more comfortable . . . just don't know" (USG investigative manager).

Summary

Mobile technologies appear to be able to improve pre-hiring processes, yet challenges remain to integrating them into SSC processes. Although such technologies are theoretically available for use, the lack of guidance, policy, and strategy aligning specific mobile technologies to SSC pre-hire stages may be preventing more robust implementation.

Interviewees from several organizations that have vetting responsibilities reported that mobile technologies could improve PV in multiple ways, including rapid acquisition of information from other organizations (e.g., courts), improving candidate experience, and increasing workforce diversity. These interviewees also listed challenges to adopting mobile technology, such as lack of workforce training or clarity about how long pandemic-era flexibility may endure. The most prominent challenge cited was a lack of clear guidance for how such technology should be used.

Overall, some interviewees from government agencies suggested that hiring flexibilities have greatly enabled virtual screening and hiring processes. Traditional in-person methods (e.g., identity verification, fingerprinting, signatures) were successfully transferred to the virtual realm over the course of the pandemic. However, some interviewees expressed concern that the USG will revert to traditional processes as pandemic restrictions are lifted. Nearly all our interviewees noted that the COVID-19 pandemic offers a useful case study to generate support for integrating mobile technology into vetting processes going forward.

CHAPTER 4

Relevant Practices in Hiring and Screening in the Private Sector

Overview

This chapter provides an overview of our discussions with private-sector organizations. First, we detail our approach to the private-sector interviews, which differs from our approach to the discussions with USG personnel described in Chapter 3.[1] Next, we describe our observations from our private-sector interview discussion, noting potentially relevant practices for the USG SSC community where available. Finally, we highlight some additional characteristics that the USG might consider as it seeks to modernize vetting practices within the context of a hybrid work environment.

Approach to Private-Sector Interviews

This section describes how we selected and interviewed our private-sector SMEs, how we analyzed the information elicited from our discussions, and what limitations we note with overall data collection. Our sponsor requested that the RAND team seek individuals with prior or current hiring expertise across four industries, preferably the technological, financial, biopharmaceutical, and gaming (i.e., casino) industries, to provide unique mobile hiring and screening insights that may have applicability to USG screening processes and share similar position-based risks. For example, a technology or biopharma organization might be concerned with employee access to intellectual property (IP) or other types of proprietary technology. A financial or gaming-based organization might be concerned with a variety of additional risks, including digital access to company financials or physical (proximity-based) risk to U.S. currency. Although our team was unable to connect with screening personnel in the gaming industry, we were able to locate an individual within the energy sector who has responsibilities for screening candidates for a small start-up company.[2] While energy-

---

[1] Our interview protocols for both populations are included in Appendix A at the end of this report.

[2] Our team made numerous attempts to locate security and hiring personnel at several prominent casinos during the course of research.

sector risks may not share direct comparison to the gaming industry, we suggest that risks associated with hiring individuals into small companies can add additional value beyond traditional or well-established organizations.[3] Table 4.1 summarizes the industries of the interviewees we spoke with and highlights some of the unique screening and hiring process characteristics across each of the sectors examined, which are discussed in more detail throughout this chapter.

We sought out interviewees across these four industries who have a variety of hiring and screening experiences to provide a more robust data comparison. Some interviewees were able to speak to the screening and hiring processes for more than one private-sector industry; for example, one individual we spoke with held several previous positions across the financial sector. If an individual held different postings throughout their career and was able to relay different types of risk considerations pertinent to this research, those experiences are indicated in Table 4.1 below by letter, number, and organizational size by personnel (e.g., A1, A2). These indicators denote that the information and subsequent analysis is derived from SME experience across different organizations.

TABLE 4.1

Private-Sector Industry Interview Snapshot

	Technology	Finance	Energy	Biopharmaceutical
Size of organization	(H1) ~1,000,000 (H2) ~70,000 (H3) ~4,500	(B1) ~200,000 (B2) ~15,000– 20,000	(A1) ~20 (start-up)	(A2) ~250 (start-up)
Risk factors and considerations	IP, source code, customers and investors, branding	Physical proximity to currency, privileged investment information, fraud, branding	Investment and external stakeholder relationships, insider and infrastructure-based threats	Physical proximity to controlled substance or chemicals, proprietary information
Types of mobile technology deployed	Video interviews, open-source or internet metadata collection, ATS, candidate texting or SMS	Video interviews, virtual aptitude testing	Video interviews, ATS, use of third-party pre-screening software	Video interviews
Other unique characteristics	Employees expected to rotate frequently and bring company knowledge to other organizations; extensive use of in-house referrals	Mass-screening to create candidate pools for high-turnover positions	Risk of hiring "wrong" person in smaller organization	Extended probationary periods as additional form of OTJ and coworker vetting

NOTE: ATS = applicant tracking system; OTJ = on-the-job.

---

[3] For example, hiring the "wrong" person into a company with only 20 staff may well have more severe repercussions hiring such a person into an organization with 20,000 staff.

The RAND team also sought informal discussions with two mobile technology vendors who provide a variety of digital services to aid organizational pre-employment screening. Each of the vendors was selected according to the types of unique candidate screening factors that each platform provides to its customer base. One vendor was selected because of platform capabilities designed to screen virtual candidate interview responses against specialized repositories that contain previously recorded "high-performer" responses. The other vendor was selected for its platform capabilities designed to screen candidates through virtual skill-based testing to develop specialized risk profiles (see Table 4.2). While there are a variety of vendors that perform services for organizations seeking to hire staff, the vendors we chose to contact were selected because of their established approach to virtual candidate vetting (e.g., informed by behavioral research).

We designed the structure of our private-sector interview protocol to elicit relevant vetting practices and other unique approaches that may add value to existing USG SSC processes. Interview topics included the following:

- Organizational details (e.g., types of high-demand personnel and associated skillsets)
- Prominent or unique types of organizational risk (e.g., types of employees that may present institutional risks or categorizations of assets that a company seeks to protect through initial vetting programs)
- Organizational measures to mitigate risk during the hiring stage (e.g., organizational-specific screening practices, skill-based testing, additional vetting measures once hired)
- Integration of mobile and desktop technologies during pre-hire interviews (e.g., characteristics of platforms used, associated challenges and enablers, platform-result adjudication)

TABLE 4.2

Vendor Platform Characteristics

	Vendor 1	Vendor 2
Types of mobile technology deployed	• Asynchronous video interviews • ML/language libraries to assess candidate's propensity for success	• Asynchronous video interviews • ML • Online risk-taking games
Types of screening implemented	• Dependability, reliability, conscientiousness (scenarios) • I/O psychology team works with hiring managers to determine position requirements	• Focused on "soft skills" • Assesses for organizational and cultural fit or risk tolerance
Other unique characteristics	• Platform assesses candidate factors that are "indicative of trust" • Language libraries updated on annual basis	• Aimed at entry-level positions to identify future career pathways and improve retention • Online game testing pre-employment, then again at six months

NOTE: I/O = industrial organization.

- Mobile platform efficiency and effectiveness (e.g., cost-per-hire considerations, platform metrics, how platforms integrate within overall hiring process).

The semistructured nature of our interview instrument allowed our team to compare findings across each of the private-sector organizations with which we spoke while also providing the flexibility to further explore unique hiring practices during our conversations (for a full listing of our private-sector interview questions, see Appendix A).

Our analysis of the interviews included a cross-comparison of organizational hiring practices, risk categorizations, risk mitigation techniques, and unique characteristics of platforms used to vet prospective hires.[4] Private-sector interview findings were also socialized during our workshop with PV and HR SMEs to further explore and validate our interview discussion data. Our overall findings across each of the organizations we spoke with are summarized in the preceding section.

Our interview data collection effort faced some limitations. First, this exploratory effort engaged a limited sample of private-sector organizations. Findings relayed in this section are therefore limited to our discussions with a single organization in a respective sector and may not be illustrative of how other organizations might approach candidate screening. Second, we were unable to contact some organizations because of factors associated with pandemic constraints (e.g., on-site travel). Both limitations could narrow the scope of inferences we are able to make across each of the sectors examined. Finally, comparing the private-sector screening process to the USG screening process presented some challenges as the USG continues to overhaul vetting programs through the TW 2.0 initiative. However, we believe the findings (and overall suggestions that appear in this report) can provide value to such programs and processes as initiatives are implemented.

Energy-Sector Discussion

Setting the Scene

Our discussion with the energy sector included a start-up organization that is actively seeking to build its baseline workforce. This organization hired its first 15 individuals between January and March 2022 and planned to hire an additional six to seven employees over the next year. The SME we spoke with at this energy start-up also managed screening processes at a pharmaceutical company and has previous experience conducting investigations for the USG. While this organization may not have direct comparability with larger USG entities, we learned that the risk of hiring the "wrong" individual in smaller organizations may

---

[4]   Our research team chose not to employ qualitative coding software due to the small n-population represented in our data.

present unique hiring considerations not commonly accounted for in existing USG vetting processes.[5]

Unique Risk Factors

Newly formed organizations face a variety of constraints that may be exacerbated if prospective hires are vetted only for factors associated with trust.[6] While trust-related factors may become more relevant as organizations continue to grow, initial hiring considerations for newly formed organizations must focus on hiring individuals that (1) will not "waste" constrained organizational resources; (2) have the ability to deploy tools or skills in line with their resume; and (3) will not damage the reputation of a newly formed company that typically retains a fragile stakeholder base.[7] Therefore, traditional security-based methods of employment screening may not address the types of factors needed to enable success within newly formed companies.

Types of Technology Deployed

Initial applicant screening for this energy start-up company includes a mix of virtual (video) and in-person interviews to determine the efficiency and effectiveness risk factors presented in the preceding section and to determine overall cultural fit. While most junior positions are screened through video platforms such as Zoom, all senior-level hires are interviewed onsite.

This organization also uses project management software to collate candidate information (e.g., resume data, cover letters, writing samples) and recruiter information (e.g., where the candidate is located, field notes) and to depict overall timelines that indicate where candidates are in the hiring process and provide alerts to both the hiring manager and the candidate.[8] Hiring and onboarding processes are typically blended together to ensure consistent communications with prospective hires.[9]

This organization uses a third-party recruitment firm to generate initial candidate leads and conducts initial screening to ensure that candidates meet minimum position requirements. Once candidates have been "pre-vetted" by the third-party recruiter, the hiring orga-

---

[5]   The chief data officer at an energy start-up with previous USG vetting experience (who previously worked on employee hiring and vetting at a small biotech start-up) noted that "at a startup with low numbers, you find that most senior people are involved with interacting with almost every person every day. . . . they have to work well with everybody" and will be directly affected by each new hire.

[6]   Such factors might include position-based risks (e.g., access to IT systems) and individual-based risk (e.g., chemical dependency or other alcohol-related issues left untreated).

[7]   Our energy-sector SME stated that "what you don't want to do is hire people that are causing you to lose or waste time. . . . are they going to show up and do work quickly and mesh with the team? . . . Right now we are just focused on not losing time" (chief data officer at energy start-up, previous USG vetting experience).

[8]   Our SME did not refer to this software as an ATS, though it appears to share many of the same characteristics.

[9]   However, our SME indicated that the objectives of the hiring and onboarding processes are different and require different forms of messaging to ensure successful transition periods.

nization conducts additional virtual interviews to ensure alignment with organizational needs and culture.

Other Types of Screening Implemented

Behavioral-based interview methods are frequently combined in virtual candidate interviews to gauge expected future performance.[10] Such questions may include the use of hypothetical scenarios intended to gauge problem-solving abilities, to understand "core motivations," to assess "coachability" once on the job, or to probe specific aspects of a resume if there are frequent gaps or changes in employment history.[11] However, our SME noted that it is difficult to determine whole-of-person considerations during 45-minute virtual interviews because candidates do not "have a chance to make an [on the job] mistake in real-time" and therefore require additional screening during the onboarding phase.

The "hall-file" serves as an additional vetting mechanism once candidates are onboarded; that is, personal interactions, passing comments, and observed actions and work processes may be reported to the hiring manager for additional employment considerations.[12] The hiring managers at this start-up company developed a series of 10 to 15 questions that are used to assess new-hire personalities and to gauge the speed of company adjustment and acculturation. Our interviewee noted that this method may be easier to achieve at smaller organizations, but that larger organizations might keep onboarding teams "on the hook" for continuous evaluation during probationary periods, not only to assess whether the individual displays expected workplace behaviors, but also to assist new hires who may be struggling in their new positions.[13]

Our discussion also revealed use of extended probationary periods to allow additional monitoring and evaluation of new hires. The use of the extended probationary period may also allow additional monitoring of employees (e.g., access to IT systems or company email) that are inaccessible during the pre-hire stage.[14] Our interviewee also suggested that extended

---

[10] The chief data officer at an energy start-up with previous USG vetting experience noted that the organization uses techniques similar to methods employed by the FBI.

[11] Our energy-sector interviewee noted that one recent candidate appeared overly concerned with levels of compensation during the "core motivation" portion of the interview, which did not fit well with the overall organizational culture focused on climate change issues. Our interviewee also noted that the use of LinkedIn to view overall hiring trends within specific sectors may prompt additional questions during the interview stage; for example, if the energy sector appears to have numerous job openings, but a candidate has been unable to secure employment, this may offer an additional course of questioning to elicit factors outside of traditional "trust"-based screening.

[12] Not to say that all feedback in this process is negative, but rather that this process may be used to "catch" people doing things "right" as well.

[13] The chief data officer at an energy start-up with previous USG vetting experience suggested calling this process *talent optimization* rather than CV.

[14] Primarily because of privacy considerations and other protections afforded to candidates outlined in Chapter 3 (e.g., APA).

probationary periods should focus on ensuring that new employees have the support needed to excel in their new positions because employment terminations can affect staff morale.

SME Recommendations for Future USG Vetting

Our energy-sector SME provided three suggestions for the USG to consider as it modernizes its vetting practices. First, the use of an extended probationary period would allow departments and agencies to implement additional modes of vetting (e.g., CV, in-person observation) that are unachievable in the pre-hire stage.[15] Next, the USG might consider increasing data collection on existing high-performing individuals to create a baseline for testing and questioning in-process candidates. Finally, our interviewee suggested that the USG should consider moving to motivation-based vetting, which may illuminate additional factors for adjudication (e.g., high interest in compensation) beyond traditional trust-based screening measures.

Financial Sector Discussion

Setting the Scene

Our discussion with the financial sector was with an individual who has held multiple senior-level positions across U.S. financial institutions with over 200,000 employees and several other SES positions across the USG. This individual's positions at financial institutions included risk management and financial crime responsibilities. The interviewee's USG responsibilities included the management of strategic planning for technology investment.

Unique Risk Factors

Employees may present several unique risks to financial institutions. Aside from the ever-present position-based risk to physical cash flows (e.g., tellers), financial institutions must contend with various levels of fraud (both internally and externally), access to IT infrastructure that protects currency exchange, and threats to international reputation to maintain a stakeholder base. Hiring for senior-level positions may introduce other types of individual-based risk, such as conflicts of interest (e.g., investments across other domestic or international financial institutions) that could affect or influence strategic investment portfolios.[16] Financial institutions also expect certain levels of organizational risk dependent on the type of position being filled. For example, traditional teller-based jobs are expected to turn over at high rates, whereas mid-to-senior–level hires may need to be provided with increased compensation for retention purposes.

---

[15] We note that this may be difficult across DoD entities because Congress repealed a two-year probationary period in Section 1106 of NDAA for FY 2022, which goes into effect December 31, 2022 (Pub. L. 117-81, 2021).

[16] Financial-firm consultant with previous USG SES experience.

Types of Technology Deployed

The financial sector deploys various tools to assist candidate vetting in the pre-hire stage, dependent on the type of position being filled. Many financial institutions rely on third-party vetting to perform basic criminal history vetting.[17] However, organizations also deploy tools with the ability to search social media feeds, online videos, or blogs routinely in tandem with the interview process. The use of LinkedIn to understand candidate affiliations, verify employment history, and understand networks provides an additional level of vetting while also allowing financial institutions to see if any existing employees may have worked with or know the candidate under scrutiny.[18] Some positions within the financial sector also require use of tools that can quickly screen for state licensing, such as verifying up-to-date Certified Public Accountant certifications and practice hours. Senior-level hires are expected to turn over personal financial statements and related documents that are further vetted with specific electronic tools to ensure that the candidate is not in a period of financial stress that could cause access issues once they are hired. Additionally, senior-level hires may receive further family-affiliation vetting to protect against conflicts of interest that may include the use of the other digital tools identified in this section.

While AI applications are fairly new, some financial institutions are exploring their use to identify open-position characteristics and the types of skillsets and training that may help individuals succeed at their job. Firms are also exploring the use of AI to proactively identify internal candidates for open positions, although the use of this technology remains in the exploratory phase.[19]

Other Types of Screening Implemented

Many organizations within the financial sector have been moving toward mass-screening to address the abundance of high-turnover positions. Mechanisms for mass-screening include the following:

1. maintaining a database of vetted candidates who were not selected for employment
2. using automated applicant processing software to remove candidacy for those who do not meet basic requirements
3. dropping traditional four-year degree requirements for some positions (e.g., tech-based) that may have more relevant certifications (e.g., cybersecurity).[20]

---

[17] Some financial consultant positions will require criminal history background checks in response to client needs; if the consultant refuses to undergo a background check, the consultant may simply be switched to serving other clients.

[18] Existing employees who have experience with a candidate may be prompted to provide comments that are reviewed along with other hiring materials.

[19] Financial-firm consultant with previous USG SES experience.

[20] Our financial SME stated that, "if I am looking at an entry-level position, someone who got a certification in cybersecurity from a reputable place can be just as effective as someone coming out of college with

Curating a database of pre-screened candidates allows hiring managers to perform outreach to candidates (who have already been vetted by the organization) about new positions that they qualify for. The use of a pre-screened database also helps financial organizations understand whether candidates have obtained any additional training or certification since applying, and to gauge whether they are still interested in working for the organization.[21]

Some organizations are also identifying candidate hobbies during the interview stage as a way to understand whether there may be other positions that may interest the candidate, and to identify areas in which a candidate may show aptitude (an ability to learn) toward achieving success in alternate career paths.[22]

SME Recommendations for Future USG Vetting

Our financial-sector SME provided a series of suggestions for consideration as the USG modernizes SSC practices in a hybrid environment. First, the USG might consider defining and developing metrics to address what success "looks like" for a virtual-based employee. Our SME suggested that most job descriptions are written based on traditional in-office values, and those are the values that candidates are vetted against during interviews. However, the USG has not yet defined what success may look like for an employee who works remotely and therefore may be vetting the future workforce against outdated criteria.[23]

As we heard in our interview with the energy-sector representative, the use of an extended probationary period may decrease overall hiring timelines and allow for additional vetting mechanisms that are prohibited in the pre-hiring stage. The financial sector routinely hires on probationary periods advisors and consultants who are transferred to full-time positions after meeting certain internal criteria.

Working in a hybrid environment presents new risks to the USG; while existing SSC forms (e.g., SF-86) include entries for friends and neighbors, roommates, family, and other living situations, working remotely may present new types of organizational risk. Non-USG employee proximity to phone calls, computer screens, or other privileged access could be

---

a cybersecurity degree. . . . In some of those areas it moves so fast that I would almost rather take someone with the near-term certification" (financial-firm consultant with previous USG SES experience).

[21] Our financial SME noted that time-to-hire calculations were significantly improved for organizations that maintained databases that included this type of information.

[22] For example, if a candidate applies to be a bank teller at an organization and lists "chef" as a hobby as part of the application process—and that organization was also searching for a chef—that could save time in searching for additional personnel.

[23] Our interviewee noted that, "It is not appropriate to hold someone accountable for something for which you've set no expectations. If I am hiring someone that will physically come into the office, I will get to observe their body language and how well they address or interact with other people and get to see and observe different types of things. . . . when people work in the office they learn from their peers. . . . they check in on people to see how they are doing, someone can get up and walk to someone. . . . in a remote environment, the job interview is very much about the personal skills, [since] you're not testing their work habits [and so may have to] look at their [curriculum vitae] for some of that . . . looking for indicators about how they handle their activities professionally" (financial-firm consultant with previous USG SES experience).

readily available given new realities presented in a hybrid work environment. The government might explore what publicly available data may exist on property records that could facilitate investigations.

Our interviewee also suggested that the USG might consider revisiting job-posting descriptions to ensure continued alignment with appropriate risk categorizations and needed qualifications. Our interviewee noted that in 2008, the USG posted a counter-finance job opening requiring cryptocurrency experience; the position remained open for an extended period, since bitcoin (and other related currencies) had appeared in use only one month prior. The interviewee also noted that the move to remote work has led to the re-examination and re-categorization of several traditional roles that were previously categorized as high-risk, which now may foster a more diverse virtual workforce for USG consideration; however, it was unclear to our interviewee whether such re-categorizations have occurred across other agencies and departments.

Technology Discussion

Setting the Scene

Our technology (sometimes referred to as *big-tech*) industry interviewee had senior-level USG experience working foundational cybersecurity efforts under former Secretary of Defense Robert Gates and as a risk consultant for four major (7,000–200,000 employees) technology firms. Consultant responsibilities included developing cybersecurity-based frameworks to protect IP, constructing pre- and post-hiring company vetting programs, and helping to integrate vetting data with organizational hiring needs.

Risk Factors and Considerations

Categories of risks posed within the technology industry share many of the same qualities as USG position-based risks. IP theft, foreign adversary access to unique platforms or code, supply-chain intrusion, and vendor trustworthiness all play a prominent role across the technology industry. Companies are also becoming increasingly concerned with employee use of social media, which may rapidly damage a company's international reputation or cause other forms of embarrassment that may lead to loss of technology users, loss of investment, or loss of other stakeholders that would disrupt organizational operations.

Types of Technology Deployed

Companies within the technology sector place high value on in-house recommendations and existing employee referrals, which can provide savings in recruiting costs and additional costs associated with finding (targeting) potential employees.[24] Some organizations have deployed platforms to help facilitate candidate referrals, including one system that provides

---

[24] Our interviewee noted that "a good recruiter, once they find someone doing well at an organization, they will hire all of their friends as long as they continue to be good recommendations" (senior hiring and screening consultant for several prominent technology companies).

a scoring mechanism to boost recruitment visibility based on internally developed metrics for success.[25]

Technology organizations had been using video-interview platforms since before the pandemic onset, though their use has increased over the past two years.[26] Pre–COVID-19, several organizations tended to use VI as an initial screening mechanism, though the final interview would be conducted in person, especially for senior-level hires.[27] Organizations now conduct all levels of interviews (e.g., junior staff, senior-level) within the virtual environment and maintain in-person interviews only for *C-suite* (e.g., CEOs, CFOs) hires. C-suite personnel may be asked to give specific presentations on risk management or privacy measures during the hiring process, providing an additional layer of scrutiny in the pre-hire stage. While some companies have begun to calculate candidate "acquisition costs," many have not yet implemented cost-per-hire assessments to compare efficiency gains from the move to virtual interviewing.

However, use of virtual platforms is not without its own set of risks. Zoom, Microsoft Teams, Jabber, and Slack can present several cybersecurity concerns. For example, such platforms are not able to protect PII that is transmitted in platform text or chat boxes. Recordings of candidate interviews and active "session bombing" may also occur, which can affect candidate trust in hiring processes.[28]

Other Types of Screening Implemented

The technology industry has experimented with monitoring LinkedIn profiles to gauge prospective candidate pool interests, skills, and locations, though such practices have not been formally instituted owing to a variety of privacy concerns and possible public-relations repercussions.[29] Employment social-networking sites, such as LinkedIn, have also started to close external access to platform application programming interfaces (APIs) to prevent individuals from being able to run program codes or scripts that could jeopardize the user base.[30] Technological organizations also use orientation periods to determine cultural fit, social assimila-

---

[25] The senior hiring and screening consultant for several prominent technology companies noted that while "this means that some underqualified people will get bumped to the top of the queue, hiring managers serve as an additional vetting mechanism to ensure job-relevant qualifications and certifications."

[26] Our interviewee also noted that use of virtual interviews also tends to put candidates more at ease during questioning and can provide more flexibility in scheduling interviews for both candidates and recruiters.

[27] Senior hiring and screening consultant for several prominent technology companies.

[28] For example, see Rosanna Xia, Howard Blume, and Luke Money, "USC, School Districts Getting 'Zoom-Bombed' with Racist Taunts, Porn as They Transition to Online Meetings," *Los Angeles Times*, March 25, 2020.

[29] If a company were using this practice and were subsequently "outed" as monitoring prospective hires, for example.

[30] For example, see Darrell Etherington, "LinkedIn Battens Down the Hatches on API Use, Limiting Full Access to Partners," *TechCrunch*, February 12, 2015.

tion, and as a method to ensure that technical competencies listed on resumes have not been "inflated" to gain entry.[31]

SME Recommendations for Future USG Vetting

Our technology SME provided two recommendations that may assist the USG in modernizing its vetting practices within the mobile context. First, our interviewee suggested that existing online e-QIP platforms should build in automated adjudication methods to ensure that information entered is valid. Not only would this assist candidates in avoiding the need to look up additional information (e.g., zip codes), but automated adjudication could also reduce overall hiring timelines that may have choke-points caused by incomplete or inaccurate candidate-provided information. Our interviewee noted that moving e-QIP to a cloud-based architecture could also allow field investigators to interact with candidates on a real-time basis (i.e., e-QIP–based chat boxes), to clarify entries or to provide additional data as needed to complete investigations without the need to consult additional information systems.[32]

Our SME also noted that there are a variety of open-source and deep-web–based tools that may be more useful for candidate vetting than traditional SF-86– (or SF-85)–based vetting forms.[33] One company has developed a series of organizational-specific risk indicators that are used as a filtering mechanisms once the open-source data collection is complete.[34] Open-source metadata collection efforts are also not subject to Fourth Amendment protections, which can provide some flexibility around other legal considerations in the pre-hire stage.

Discussion with Technology Vendor A

Setting the Scene (Organization Background)

One technology vendor our research team spoke with provides a variety of mobile screening services to the USG and private sector.[35] Organizations primarily perform outreach with this vendor to rapidly identify candidate pools with relevant skills and abilities, as a mass pre-hire method to screen multiple candidates against specific job openings, and to save costs associ-

---

[31] The orientation period is also used to improve subsequent recruiting and hiring for future candidates. At the end of the orientation period, new employees fill out a survey that asks specific questions about their hiring experience that are operationalized to revamp existing hiring processes. The surveys are also tied to recruiter compensation (e.g., if the candidate had a good experience).

[32] Our SME indicated that U.S. Department of Health and Human Services, Office of Planning, Research and Evaluation may provide a specific case study for how to handle sensitive PII on mobile platforms. Our interviewee also noted that speaking with various USG statistical agencies (FedRAMP-approved) may provide additional ideas for how to build in mobile communications to complete data capture.

[33] Especially for emerging workforce populations.

[34] Nondisclosure agreements prevented our SME from being able to further discuss this effort.

[35] Of note, the vendor is not aware of any USG departments or agencies using the platform to make security clearance decisions, but it is being used to "inform suitability-based work" (vice president of mobile technology firm).

ated with recruiter or candidate travel. This vendor also provides customer relationship management (CRM) software to assist in matching candidates with hiring organizations. The CRM tool retains online chat functionality that can send job alerts to candidates depending on the type of skills or qualifications uploaded into the system.

Types of Screening Services Provided

The first technology vendor we spoke with provides asynchronous VI platforms that include a series of structured interview questions (questions are developed in tandem with hiring managers) and automated candidate workflow dashboards that provide hiring managers with a daily overview of candidate progress within the organization's hiring pipeline.

This technology platform also provides numerical candidate scoring to highlight overall job fit.[36] Candidate scores are derived from use of natural language processing (NLP) software. The NLP software contains predetermined language-use libraries that house candidate remarks, organizational leadership statements, or other words that may serve as indicators for future success at a particular organization. Candidates with the highest scores are ranked and referred by the platform to hiring managers, who may follow up with real-time virtual or in-person interviews.[37] Language-use models are revalidated on an annual basis to ensure continued validity (e.g., Are the candidates who are being hired successful in their new positions?) and have instituted research teams to assess formation of bias within both the structured questions and the language-libraries in use.[38] The technology company also works closely with hiring managers to ensure that job postings and descriptions remain current and aligned with the platform-based job competencies. Some government and private-sector organizations may provide their own custom language-libraries for platform assessment. The Department of Labor and OPM's Multipurpose Occupational Systems Analysis Inventory–Close-Ended (MOSAIC) have provided customized job categorizations and descriptions that have been used to assess candidates.[39]

The vendor we spoke with also highlighted that although its technology platform does not screen according to factors associated with "trust," it does focus on factors relative to a candidate's "dependability, reliability, and conscientiousness," which, they suggested, could

---

[36] Vice president of mobile technology firm.

[37] Our vendor interview indicated that it hires panels of industrial and organizational psychologists to develop rubrics for success (e.g., what a "good answer looks like," or what sorts of combinations of words may be indicative of "good teamwork"). This company had attempted to collect nonverbal behavior as part of the overall scoring assessment but found that such data created too many anomalies for accurate interpretation.

[38] Recalibration of the platform can take months, because any refinement is based on hiring-organization provision of employee data.

[39] The USG may also have department-specific IO psych teams collaborate with the vendor to develop tailored position indicators of success. For more on MOSAIC, see OPM, "Policy, Data, Oversight: OPM's MOSAIC Studies and Competencies," undated-e.

be indicative of trust.[40] This platform also uses emotional- and behavioral-based–intelligence online games that provide some indication of the candidate's risk propensity.

Platform Enablers and Challenges

One primary enabler for this platform is that video-based interviews (and the associated credentials needed to access the video platform) serve as a security layer to ensure that the "right" person is answering the questions posed. The vendor suggests that video interviews can provide additional layers of visibility to ensure candidate identities not otherwise afforded through traditional phone-based interviews.[41]

While this platform provides several advantages that could assist USG mobile-vetting efforts, the use of such technology also presents several challenges that could limit its utility. This platform has experienced issues related to "script-sharing," where one candidate may pass the structured-interview questions to a friend or acquaintance in an attempt to gain advantage over others. This vendor also reported that respondents may be "coached" in real time by someone off camera, which can greatly skew interview results.[42]

Recommendations for Future USG Vetting

Our first technology vendor suggested that the USG should consider revising the length of time that job postings remain open across various hiring sites (e.g., USAJobs) and developing new government-hiring websites that could cater to a larger audience. The vendor suggested that current government job postings may appear for only a short time, reducing the necessary visibility to generate a larger, more diverse candidate pool. The vendor also suggested that a new USG hiring website should also contain built-in CRM software to answer candidate questions, proactively send announcements to candidates who have uploaded resumes or other certifications, and retain an ability to mass-screen applications against additional postings that the candidate may not be aware of.

The first vendor also suggested that the USG could make increased use of SMS texting with prospective employees to aid in initial vetting efforts. However, since candidates may be using a non-USG approved device (which could present a variety of access issues), initial outreach efforts would likely need to move to an encrypted messaging service having characteristics similar to Telegram, Signal, or WhatsApp.

---

[40] Vice president of mobile technology firm.

[41] One interviewee noted that "it's hard to fake a video interview." Another on the group call suggested that candidates are "less likely to lie" when being recorded, since those results could be verified in follow-on investigations (vice president of mobile technology firm).

[42] The vendor reported that they have some "analytic capabilities" to catch candidates attempting to receive real-time advice off-camera.

Discussion with Technology Vendor B

Setting the Scene (Organization Background)

The second technology vendor we spoke with provides a variety of pre-screening services to assess candidates through a talent acquisition workflow lens.[43] This vendor provides services to a wide variety of domestic and international customers categorized within the Fortune 2000 (sometimes referred to as the "Global 2000").[44] The platform offered by this vendor shares some characteristics with that of the first vendor we spoke with but has several unique characteristics that may further assist USG efforts to implement future mobile screening practices.[45] For example, this platform not only identifies and assesses initial applicants but is also used to aid in the retention of existing employees by highlighting additional organization roles where an employee might be successful.[46]

Types of Screening Services Provided

Like the first vendor we spoke with, our second vendor employs teams of I/O psychologists to work with hiring organizations to develop metrics and language-use indicators for success. The platform offered by this vendor is premised on the ability to predict whether an applicant will be a good fit for the hiring organization. Prediction accuracy is based on ML analysis of candidate responses to skill-based and aptitude-based tests. Candidate responses are compared with other existing employee responses to determine matching percentages. Initial candidate responses to administered tests are compared against the same candidate's responses one year later to improve platform algorithms.[47]

Platform Enablers and Challenges

Much like the discussion on the first vendor platform, this second platform does not specifically screen for candidate trust; rather, this platform is designed to discover candidate "soft skills" that may be indicative of position-based success or aptitude to learn specific job-based skills. The platform also hosts a variety of games aimed at identifying a candidate's tolerance for risk (or *risk-threshold*) that is combined with soft-skill testing to produce an aggregate

---

[43] For more on talent acquisition processes, see Society for Human Resource Management, *Talent Acquisition: A Guide to Understanding and Managing the Recruitment Process*, 2016.

[44] Senior data scientist for a mobile technology firm.

[45] Note that the discussion in this section is based on a 25-minute conversation with our second vendor and therefore is comparatively shorter than the other sections in this chapter.

[46] This games-based platform is also able to identify particular training pathways that could improve existing employee retention over time.

[47] An external entity provides an additional layer of ML and AI oversight to vet algorithms for various types of bias.

candidate score.[48] Risk-tolerance thresholds and scoring are derived from the vendor's team of behavior and psychology specialists.

One limiting factor of this technology is that the platform is not currently available on mobile devices, which may cause some accessibility issues for prospective employees. The need for a desktop machine or other onsite terminal offered through this company may decrease the overall applicant pool or otherwise inhibit the testing of a more diverse population. Another limiting factor that surfaced from our discussion is that the testing may not immediately match a candidate with a specific job but rather demonstrate the potential for a candidate to excel in a variety of generalized occupations, which could present some challenges to USG hiring organizations seeking to fill specific positions.

Recommendations for Future USG Vetting

Our second technology vendor noted two key factors that could assist in modernizing the SSC process. First, that USG organizations might seek to screen for *soft skills* (e.g., communication, aptitude for learning), which could provide value beyond establishing traditional measures of trust. Measuring soft skills through mobile applications may also highlight additional skills or interests that USG organizations could use to help candidates identify specific training or career pathways that align with their career goals. Second, using mobile risk-based games could assist the USG in identifying a candidate's propensity for risk, which may help USG hiring managers in rank-ordering candidates.[49]

Private-Sector Interview Summary

This section briefly summarizes our observations gained through the interviews with private-sector organizations and our informal discussions with technology vendors. We present these observations at a strategic level to facilitate comparison between the private sector and the USG.[50]

Observation 1: There are many legal and policy challenges to mobile-vetting use in the hiring stage. U.S. private-sector organizations are bound by the same set of legal statutes that may prohibit various types of mobile platform vetting in the pre-hire stage for the USG. For example, companies and organizations may not collect a candidate's digital information (collection, transmission, and storage are all problematic) that would violate Fourth Amend-

---

[48] For example, one game focused on tolerance for risk depicts a balloon slowly filling with air; the more the balloon inflates, the more fake virtual currency the candidate will receive.

[49] Risk scores could be aligned with existing position-based risk considerations, or along the new SSC tiering structure as part of the TW 2.0 initiative.

[50] A more granular-level view of these observations is presented in the preceding sections of this chapter.

ment protections, the ECPA, or the Privacy Act of 1974.[51] Several private-sector organizations have instituted extended probationary periods as a method to introduce additional vetting mechanisms beyond initial interview stages. For example, an organization may have internal data monitoring policies for employees that can be deployed when a candidate accepts a probationary assignment. Extended probationary periods (which may include onboarding and other types of job-acculturation) for newly hired employees may also include additional evaluation by coworkers, managers, or other in-office peers who may report derogatory information back to hiring managers. However, such periods may also be used to improve organizational hiring and onboarding processes through candidate feedback (e.g., surveys).

The move to a hybrid or remote work environment has proved equally challenging for the private sector. New hires entering organizations during the pandemic have not been readily observable by peers and coworkers during probationary periods, making the assessment of skills, competencies, and other behaviors that may indicate risk to the organization difficult to perform. The private sector is attempting to address this issue through more-frequent informal virtual interactions between newly hired staff and existing employees in similar job positions.

Observation 2: Some organizations in the private sector have deployed several innovative screening methods to meet organizational hiring demand. While most of the candidate screening across the private sector is performed by a third-party vetting service, many organizations have adapted various forms of behavioral interview techniques into initial candidate interviews. All of the private-sector organizations we spoke with also appear to place more emphasis on cultural fit, motivations, and other soft skills (e.g., communication, teamwork, ability to problem-solve) than on a purely security focus.[52] Our interviews with mobile technology vendors validated this shift, because some private-sector organizations have increased use of their services to assess candidate soft skills, risk tolerance, and aptitude over the past two years.

Many organizations have also invested in technology platforms that can aid in the mass-screening of prospective employees. Having "pre-cleared" candidate populations has allowed the private sector to rapidly fill open positions. Some organizations have also procured ATS to function both as a situational awareness tool for hiring managers and as a method to communicate with prospective (those looking for jobs) and in-process candidates.[53]

---

[51] For more, see Damon W. Silver, "5 Key Data Privacy and Security Risks That Arise When Organizations Record Job Interviews and Strategies for Mitigating Them," *National Law Review*, Vol. XII, No. 338, April 13, 2021.

[52] This is partly an acknowledgment that employees will rotate out to other companies or firms and will likely bring company knowledge to new positions.

[53] Some ATS platforms have built-in SMS and automated email generators to alert candidates of where they are in the hiring process and additional items that may be required and to proactively search for and track others who may be interested in working at the hiring organization.

Observation 3: Technology vendors have developed several screening indicators that may amplify existing USG efforts focused solely on establishing levels of trust. Building on Observation 2, technology vendors have developed various mobile games and assessments to gauge candidate dependability, reliability, conscientiousness, and other soft skills that they suggest are indicative of overall trust. Such platforms are also able to elicit latent skills, interests, and aptitude for a variety of job opportunities that a candidate may not have initially considered.[54] Vendors routinely work with organizational hiring managers to define appropriate (relevant) job requirements and as a validation exercise to ensure that mobile assessments are producing candidates in line with organizational expectations.

Technology vendors also provide asynchronous video interview services to the private sector and the USG. Candidate responses to structured questions (developed in line with hiring managers) are analyzed against ML libraries that contain language-use examples from high performers in similar job categories.

The next section provides an overview of our workshop in which we discussed and elaborated on the themes elicited from our private-sector interviews. Although we designed the workshop to align with the prominent private-sector findings identified in this section, we also added some additional categories for discussion to ensure holistic capture of options to integrate mobile technologies into existing SSC processes.

Subject-Matter Expert Workshop Themes

Overview of Workshop

Our research team held a 90-minute workshop in April 2022 to further explore how mobile technology might improve the initial stages of the SSC process and to better understand other key factors that the USG should consider as it seeks to implement mobile platforms with future vetting processes. Workshop discussion periods were divided into six 15-minute sessions to explore these two guiding questions (see Table 4.3 for a more granular-level view of workshop proceedings). This section presents a high-level summary of the workshop discussions and relevant findings and themes by each subsection.

Workshop Theme A: Develop and Test Use-Case, Then Apply Technology

Several comments made during the first session of our workshop focused on the need to develop use-cases for mobile vetting technology. Three workshop members suggested that there are likely a wide range of technologies that could support existing pre-hire vetting processes, though their utility would depend on how the selected technology could or would be used to support hiring managers, investigators, and adjudicators.

Some group members noted that the development of use-cases might also highlight additional areas that could be enhanced through mobile technology. One participant expressed

---

[54] This may increase overall retention.

TABLE 4.3

Internal Workshop Agenda

Time	Purpose	Guiding Question(s)
2:00–2:15	• Establish project background and context • Provide brief summary of interview findings	N/A
2:15–2:30	• Establish group baseline of existing or emerging technology (both HR and vetting)	• What existing technologies could support mobile vetting? • What new or emerging technologies could support mobile vetting? • What features must the technologies have to be successful when applied to mobile vetting? What features should be avoided?
2:30–2:45	• Understand key enablers for existing SSC vetting	• How might mobile tech enable the hiring process? • How might mobile tech improve candidate experience?
2:45–3:00	• Understand key challenges to SSC implementation	• What is in the realm of the possible (legally, feasibly, ethically)? • What can "we" do? what can we not do? • Ethically, are there things that we "should and should not" do (DEIA considerations)? • What are key challenges to implementation?
3:00–3:15	• Next steps for USG implementation (general level)	• What might the USG be able to implement in the near term (1–2 years)? Mid term (3–5 years)? Long term (6–10 years)?
3:15–3:30	• Call for blue-sky ideas	• Legal and policy considerations aside, what would you want to know about a potential candidate in today's environment (e.g., new types of risks posed by hybrid work)?

NOTE: DEIA = diversity, equity, inclusion, and access.

concern that simply automating existing vetting processes might further entrench legacy processes that might be better accomplished (or enabled) by other uses of mobile technologies.[55] Instead, the USG might focus on areas in which to implement mobile platforms that can be used to "improve candidate experience" instead of solely for vetting purposes.[56] Initial steps for developing use-cases might include understanding what types of data could be made available to hiring managers, investigators, and adjudicators, and then layering supporting technologies on top of data requirements. Initial steps might also include the development of specific scenarios to identify what types of technology would be needed to address vetting requirements.[57]

---

[55] HR SME.

[56] For example, two participants noted that mobile technology may be especially useful for the PR of cleared personnel working overseas. HR SME, intelligence community (IC) SME.

[57] Some law enforcement communities are using pilot programs for vetting candidates that may serve as models for use-case development. IC SME.

Workshop participants suggested several near-term actions to assist with implementing mobile technology into USG vetting processes. First, group members with emerging-technology expertise suggested that relevant USG vetting stakeholders should develop some initial sets of scenarios or use-cases to assess adversary capabilities against proposed vetting technologies. For example, creating red teams to hack or spoof mobile data streams might reveal areas of weakness that would require alternative mitigation methods or access points to protect both the candidate and the vetting staff.[58] Workshop participants with emerging technology expertise also noted that most commercial-off-the-shelf technologies are readily available to the USG and that developing pilot programs might be a more cost-effective solution before a full rollout of any specific technology or platform. Further, the USG may already have access to some data that could provide a research baseline for developing mobile technology pilots; for example, DHS's CBP collects robust amounts of mobile screening data across border crossings that may involve collection of biometrics, facial recognition, or other identity markers that could be categorized or aligned with current vetting processes.[59] Emerging-technology participants also cautioned that any pilot program planning would also need to include appropriate legal protections and a strategy for implementation if proven successful.

Other group members with HR expertise noted that the USG might explore alternative personnel hiring systems that may already have flexibilities within them that would allow mobile technology testing and experimentation (on internal populations) to identify possibilities of using the platforms for external populations.

Workshop Theme B: Existing Technologies May Enable Vetting but Face Legal/ Empirical Obstacles

Group members with emerging-technology and behavioral expertise reported the existence of multiple technologies that could be used to aid existing vetting processes, though they repeatedly acknowledged legal or other constitutional requirements that would prevent use in the pre-hiring stage. Voice-stress analysis, linguistic interpretation, facial expression, and other voice-analysis platforms are frequently used in the financial and insurance sector to detect fraud. Online dating-service platforms are using ML algorithms to assess identity and to protect their user bases from malicious actors. Both U.S. and international airports frequently use thermal imaging to detect possible stress-related issues on a daily basis. However, use of such technologies within the USG hiring process is governed by a variety of legislative protections, including the E-Government Act, NIST, FISMA, and the APA.[60] The use of such

---

[58] One participant noted that, "I would like to see some sort of red or gray-colored actors trying to spoof and hack the new data streams, whether they are locational, reputational . . . because every time you throw in a new data stream, you have new vulnerabilities" (behavioral/emerging technology SME).

[59] A participant with legal expertise noted that pilot designers and participants would need to abide by existing USG privacy laws.

[60] Among other policies identified in Chapter 3 of this report.

technologies in the pre-hire stage also faces several empirical challenges; for example, group members felt that there simply has not been enough data collection or analysis to determine whether findings from the deployment of mobile technologies could be used as the evidentiary basis for clearance determinations.[61]

Workshop Theme C: Use of Mobile Technology May Create a More Comfortable Candidate Experience

The second workshop session was designed to discover how the use of mobile technology might best support existing vetting processes. One key theme that emerged in the conversation was increasing candidate comfort during security interview screening. Some participants with behavioral expertise commented that traditional polygraph use tends to make candidates uncomfortable and continues to face various types of scrutiny throughout the community (e.g., questions regarding validity of test results).[62] Existing mobile or remote technologies, such as the use of thermal imaging, may put candidates more at ease with their security interviewers. Behavioral SMEs noted that mobile technologies might best be used to develop initial sets of indicators that could inform subsequent vetting processes. For example, if a "Himalayan peak" registers on a mobile platform during candidate questioning, investigators might use platform data as an indicator to perform a deep dive on the answer that was provided. One group member with vetting expertise also suggested that mobile technologies that can perform deep web searches or open-source searches may greatly assist in filtering out candidates who likely would not be able to adjudicate security concerns.

Workshop Theme D: Mobile Technology Can Keep Candidates Informed

There are a variety of mobile applications that may serve to keep candidates well informed during the pre-hiring stage. One HR SME noted that the USG may be losing candidates not only to lengthy hiring timelines but also to a lack of effective communication between candidates, investigators, adjudicators, and hiring organizations. Participants suggested that many candidates may not be familiar with USG vetting processes or expectations and may not know whom to contact for additional information. Using mobile technologies (e.g., texts, chats, ATS) to enable more-effective communication between hiring organizations and candidates could lead to better hiring-process retention over time.[63]

Some workshop participants noted that the USG will need to further explore how mobile technologies will benefit both in-process candidates and those who may be considering a

---

[61] For example, our legal SME noted that "When speaking about doing something new using, for example, facial recognition, to make an employment-based judgment or security personnel-based judgment, we have to be careful because the government has to abide by rules from the APA. The APA requires the government to make decisions based on substance of evidence."

[62] One former IC professional acknowledged that making candidates uncomfortable is part of the aim during polygraph sessions but felt there were more efficient methods for determining levels of trust, including thermal imaging.

[63] Indeed, this is a key initiative outlined in the USG's TW 2.0 initiative.

career in government service. In-person fingerprinting and locating previous employment contact information or residential addresses can frustrate candidates and slow overall hiring timelines. However, most (if not all) of these basic elements of establishing candidate identity are available through other platforms (e.g., web-scrapes) and may ease the already stressful hiring processes. The use of hiring feedback forms (once hired) or the collection of data from customer experience communication platforms for those already in-process may highlight additional areas for consideration when deciding where best to deploy mobile vetting technologies.

Workshop Theme E: Vetting for Skills and Job Competencies

One HR workshop participant felt that the use of mobile technology platforms may be able to assist in vetting candidate skills and other relevant job competencies that current vetting processes do not account for, in line with our private-sector discussions. Mobile technologies, such as social virtual reality platforms, could be used to test the ability of candidates to work as part of a team or their effectiveness at group problem solving. The HR SME noted that it may be more valuable to screen candidates who work well within teams and demonstrate an ability to learn over time than to focus on "experts" who may not work well with others.[64] However, developing mechanisms to screen candidate skills and competencies will require validation against unique job categories.

Workshop Theme F: Mobile Technology Could Introduce Bias and DEIA Issues

Several participants cited several examples in which bias within mobile technologies (e.g., AI, ML) could be detrimental to USG hiring efforts. Facial recognition software, wearable trackers (e.g., Fitbits), ML language-use comparisons, and other technology that screens against an established baseline has the potential to introduce various forms of bias into vetting processes.[65] Subsequent interpretations of data provided by mobile platforms are subject to various forms of bias, including (1) *confirmation bias* (confirming pre-held values or beliefs),[66] (2) *affinity bias* (preference for individual traits that most closely resemble adjudicator characteristics),[67] or (3) *statistical discrimination* (using known identity traits to infer

---

[64] Group members cited Laszlo Bock, *Work Rules! Insights from Inside Google That Will Transform How You Live and Lead*, Twelve, 2015, to demonstrate this point.

[65] One behavioral SME noted that access to WiFi and the distribution of data-access points would limit mobile interaction with candidates who live in rural areas, or other areas across U.S. tribal territories.

[66] Olivia C. Sailors, "At the Nexus of Neoliberalism, Mass Incarceration, and Scientific Racism: The Conflation of Blackness with Risk in the 21st Century," *Tapestries: Interwoven Voices of Local and Global Identities*, Vol. 9, No. 1, Article 7, 2020.

[67] Lincoln Quillian, "Does Unconscious Racism Exist?" *Social Psychology Quarterly*, Vol. 71, No. 1, 2008; Troy Duster, "Introduction to Unconscious Racism Debate," *Social Psychology Quarterly*, Vol. 71, No. 1, 2008; David Kairys, "Unconscious Racism," *Temple Law Review*, Vol. 83, No. 4, 2011.

unobservable individual characteristics),[68] that may negatively affect a candidate's applica-tion.[69] One SME with legal expertise highlighted that any use of mobile technology data will require stringent usage protocols, DEIA training, and use of a third party to maintain vetting process objectivity.

Workshop Theme G: Mobile Technology Acceptance Will Require Cultural Shifts

The end of the first session culminated in a discussion focused on USG vetting culture. Workshop participants suggested that one of the primary challenges to incorporating tech-nology into existing vetting processes concerns vetting-staff perceptions about its efficiency and effectiveness over traditional in-person processes. While the COVID-19 pandemic may have forced many agencies and department into accepting virtual or remote forms of vetting, many departments and agencies have already begun to revert to traditional in-person vetting methods. One workshop participant noted that some agencies even ceased vetting operations during pandemic-related conditions (in effect, freezing hiring for a period of 18 months) because hiring managers and vetting staff refused to use VI platforms or other virtual-based methods to determine candidate identity.[70] Other participants noted that there may be some reservations about accepting technology given fears of job-based or position obsolescence—that traditional USG vetting jobs may be replaced by automation or virtual-based platforms. Emerging-technology and HR participants suggested that many of the cultural barriers could be mitigated by illustrating how mobile technologies could better manage vetting caseloads (process efficiency) and enable increased diversity and accessibility for candidates who may not work or live close to USG hiring organizations.

While the pandemic has enabled (or forced) some organizations to accept that some aspects of the SSC vetting process can be performed through mobile technologies (e.g., VI), partici-pants suggested that several organizations have already begun to revert to traditional in-person or paper-form-based methods of exchange as pandemic conditions have eased. Worse yet, it is unclear whether organizations actively captured best practices or lessons learned during early phases of the pandemic, which would prevent institutional learning when or if a new pandemic were to emerge. Participants with organizational and HR expertise noted that USG vetting stakeholders should be laying the foundation for organization-wide cultural shifts to relay benefits of applying mobile technologies to the existing vetting process. Such

---

[68] Dennis J. Aigner and Glen G. Cain, "Statistical Theories of Discrimination in Labor Markets," *ILR Review*, Vol. 30, No. 2, January 1977.

[69] See Sailors, 2020; Quillian, 2008; Duster, 2008; Kairys, 2011; and Aigner and Cain, 1977, as cited in Tepring Piquado, Sina Beaghley, Lisa Pelled Colabella, and Nahom M. Beyene, *Assessing the Potential for Racial Bias in the Security Clearance Process*, RAND Corporation, RR-A1201-1-v2, 2021.

[70] HR SME. One participant commented that recent interviews with one organization highlighted that it was a huge adjustment from "knocking on doors" to performing interviews on computers, and that this organization would accept only candidates that have been "eyeballed" by interviewers or investigators in-person.

a foundation might include the use of surveys to assess and address areas of concern, such as DoD's "Cyber Acceptance Survey" that is administered to gauge staff understanding of cyber-related efforts.[71]

Summary

We sought to understand relevant private-sector practices and potential lessons for the government in two ways: semistructured interviews and an expert workshop. First, at the sponsor's request, we conducted discussions with private-sector organizations in sectors relevant for government PV, including the technology, finance, and energy industries. These discussions focused on relevant vetting practices and other unique approaches that may add value to existing USG SSC processes. We also held informal discussions with two mobile technology vendors of pre-employment screening services. A few common recommendations emerged from the private-sector interviews. The first recommendation was to consider implementing an extended probationary period that could use vetting techniques unavailable in pre-hire phases. The second recommendation generally involved collecting additional data and defining metrics, including looking for publicly available (e.g., online) data that would help set a baseline for high-performing candidates and developing new metrics (e.g., based on motivation rather than only trust). A third recommendation was to periodically revisit job postings to ensure that they target qualified candidates and are aligned with requirements and risk categorizations.

Second, we conducted a workshop with SMEs to build on themes emerging in the private-sector interviews. Workshop participants suggested developing use-cases for proposed mobile technologies and ways to facilitate implementation, such as using existing government data to develop baselines for pilot studies. The participants also echoed many of the themes that private-sector interviewees raised. Participants suggested that benefits of mobile technology also included an ability to improve candidate experience, through increased communication during the hiring process. However, implementing mobile vetting technology will face legal barriers, bias concerns, and a vetting community desire to return to traditional vetting models.

---

[71] See Jackson Barnett, "Survey Finds DOD Contractors Know Little About Forthcoming Cyber Standards," *FEDSCOOP*, January 23, 2020.

CHAPTER 5

Observations, Suggestions, and Conclusions

Overview

This chapter serves as the culmination of our findings gleaned throughout each phase of this research project. The observations that appear in this chapter are evidenced through our public- and private-sector literature review, our interviews with USG vetting stakeholders, and our discussions with private-sector organizations in select industries and mobile technology vendors. The suggestions offered in this chapter reflect the output of the workshop held in April 2022 and our research team's analysis of literature and interview findings. We do not provide any particular prioritization scheme across the observations and suggestions below, since many of the recommended tasks or actions would likely occur simultaneously across the USG. However, we would suggest further alignment of our proposed suggestions with the Federal PV Guidelines, which could further reinforce (and validate) the prioritized initiatives contained therein.[1]

Observation 1: The USG has not integrated mobile technology with SSC vetting processes. While the USG does use various tools and technologies to screen and assess existing employee behavior and actions (e.g., insider threat detection, keyboard strokes) in the post-hire stage, the USG has not yet incorporated mobile technology into SSC vetting practices. Multiple USG interviewees reported that use of mobile technology in the pre-hire stage could rapidly close data-gaps that might otherwise prolong traditional vetting processes.

Although we did not evaluate the USG pre-hire process, observations from Chapter 4 highlighted some private-sector pre-hire activities that could offer benefits to the USG process. For example, some private-sector organizations use mobile technology platforms in the pre-hire stage to assess various aspects of a candidate's dependability, reliability, and conscientiousness that may serve a preliminary gate-keeping function for assessing a future employee's trustworthiness that may provide useful information for follow-up during SSC

---

[1] A recent PV Reform Quarterly Progress Update notes that the guidelines "describe the vision for creating a PV program that ensures Americans can trust the Federal workforce to protect people, property, information, and mission; and moreover, is aligned with and supportive of the Federal government's broader efforts to recruit and retain a diverse and talented workforce." Further, that the "issuance of these Guidelines represents a critical milestone on the path toward full realization of the TW 2.0 personnel vetting model." See "Personnel Vetting Reform Quarterly Progress Update FY 2022, Quarter 1," briefing slides, Performance. gov, 2022; and ODNI and OPM, "Federal Personnel Vetting Guidelines," February 10, 2022.

interviews and follow-on investigations. Interviews with private-sector organizations also emphasize use of mobile technologies to discover a candidate's latent skills, interests, and aptitude for a wide variety of job opportunities that may be helpful to long-term retention of employees who have successfully completed PV.

- **Suggestion 1.1.** The USG might seek to further define and codify mobile vetting policy and guidance. The development of mobile vetting policy would necessitate a thorough legal review of policies and procedures identified in Chapter 3 (e.g., the Privacy Act) to better understand what is in the realm of the possible. Such codification should also include strategic department and agency messaging to relay the value of mobile platforms to organizations stymied by traditional vetting culture.[2]

- **Suggestion 1.2.** The USG could capture department and agency best practices and lessons learned over the course of the pandemic to ensure that institutional knowledge of virtual vetting is not lost. Hiring flexibilities, video interviews, and other virtual vetting techniques should be captured, analyzed, and made available in anticipation of a similar future pandemic or event that could disrupt our national security personnel pipeline. This effort might include the use of surveys or other informal taskers to SSC stakeholders to allow postpandemic reflection. Seeking to accomplish this task as soon as possible would also avoid issues in staff turnover or other events that could detract from adequate knowledge management.

- **Suggestion 1.3.** The USG might consider greater formalization of virtual training for investigators—and for adjudication staff who may rely on a system of adjudication intended for in-person interviews and investigations. Our interviews suggest that, although the USG was able to conduct video interviews with prospective employees, numerous investigators struggled to address administrative issues associated with virtual connections (e.g., issues with Zoom links, reschedules). Our interviews also suggested that investigators may be relying on in-person (traditional) methods of interviewing that may not have applicability on virtual platforms.[3]

- **Suggestion 1.4.** The USG should consider developing strategic messaging across SSC stakeholders to set the foundation for future vetting cultural shifts. Conducting a cost-comparison (cost per hire assessment) of efficiencies gained during the pandemic through use of virtual platforms versus in-person screening mechanisms may assist in providing the foundation for a messaging effort.

- **Suggestion 1.5.** The USG might consider adopting some of the private-sector organizational practices that seek to uncover factors that are indicative of trust (e.g., measures of dependability, reliability, conscientiousness) that could complement existing SSC vet-

---

[2] Our USG interviews indicated that, although TW 2.0 initiatives are understood throughout the SSC community, further work may be needed to lay the foundation for a cultural shift.

[3] For example, investigators may need to consider other factors that may not be readily apparent on a video interview, such as foot-tapping or other anxious behaviors.

ting mechanisms. Adopting mobile platforms that elicit such measurements through games or other candidate assessment functions may serve as an additional gate-keeping function for employment consideration.

Observation 2: Expanding the use of mobile technologies beyond traditional vetting models could uncover additional information sources and shorten investigation timelines. As one of our workshop participants noted, the USG should not simply take an outdated process and automate it via a mobile platform. For example, the use of fingerprinting may be an outdated practice for establishing candidate identity when compared against other identity markers that are openly available. Therefore, the USG might explore additional data sources and categories (e.g., deep-web searches, open-source scrapes) that could replace traditional vetting models to avoid automation of outdated processes.

- **Suggestion 2.1.** Developing vetting scenarios and use-cases and piloting select platforms could help identify and align specific technologies to data required in the pre-hire stage. Some USG interviewees noted that many existing desktop applications could transition to a mobile environment and may offer an initial starting point for application alignment.

Observation 3: There are opportunities for the USG to adopt several private-sector hiring practices that may improve overall candidate vetting experience. Private-sector use of ATS serves two purposes; first, it provides hiring managers with increased visibility of the overall hiring pipeline and helps to identify chokepoints in the hiring process. Second, tracking software provides those in process with a better understanding of where they are in the process and can also prompt candidates to provide additional information as needed to complete the application process.[4]

- **Suggestion 3.1.** The USG could consult with federal organizations actively using ATS to explore and identify areas that may benefit the SSC process. For example, if a candidate does not have a particular form or certificate at the time of the e-QIP submission, having a system in place to alert candidate to missing information or gaps in submitted applications would proactively ease the burden on both parties.

Observation 4: Adopting mobile technology could promote a more diverse workforce in accordance with EO 14035 and consistent with related priorities for TW 2.0 implementation.[5] DEIA is a key USG hiring priority. Interviews with the USG and private sector and findings from our internal workshop noted how the use of mobile technology could generate

---

[4] At least one federal law enforcement organization has been using ATS since 2020, which has provided numerous benefits—including the ability to rapidly fill vacant positions.

[5] Joseph R. Biden, Jr., Executive Order 14035, "Executive Order on Diversity, Equity, Inclusion, and Accessibility in the Federal Workforce," June 25, 2021.

additional pools of candidates with a wide array of talents, skills, and viewpoints that may not be accessible through more-traditional methods of application and screening. However, future mobile implementation must also account for a candidate's ability to access and engage with the USG via mobile devices to create equity among candidate pools.

- **Suggestion 4.1.** The USG might seek to identify areas within the existing application and vetting process that may exclude underrepresented candidate populations and align technologies to support DEIA initiatives. For example, generating locational hiring data (for national security positions) over the past five to seven years across agencies could reveal locational heat-maps of underrepresented communities. The USG should also consider what types of technologies may or may not be accessible to certain populations (e.g., at the local, tribal, or territorial level) while at the same time ensuring that the move to mobile does not exclude potential candidates who may not have access to mobile tech.

Observation 5: Identifying metrics for success within a virtual or hybrid working environment could help to ensure that the USG is vetting for the most relevant factors. Screening candidates against criteria intended for in-office positions (e.g., *does the candidate follow senior-level instruction?*) versus emerging hybrid or remote criteria (e.g., *is the candidate self-motivated to accomplish departmental mission and objectives?*) may assist the USG in developing relevant metrics for mobile assessment. A shift from traditional in-person employees to a remote work environment may, for example, shift the locus of position-based risk assessments (trust in position) to assessing for the types of soft skills noted within our conversations with the mobile technology vendors (trust in person).[6]

- **Suggestion 5.1.** The USG could begin developing metrics (measures of performance and measures of effectiveness) for determining hybrid and remote work performance goals. Understanding criteria for "success" when working remotely will likely take various forms, dependent on department and agency missions—though such understanding will assist in developing accurate job descriptions and, therefore, more relevant screening questions. New screening factors might include an ability to complete work on time without immediate supervision (motivation and dependability), proactive use of office technology to communicate with coworkers who need assistance (conscientiousness), or a failure to report sensitive information discussed in an unclassified virtual meeting (risk propensity).
- **Suggestion 5.2.** SSC stakeholders could identify existing questions or categories of position-based screening that may not be as relevant for certain populations of the emerging hybrid or fully remote workforce. SSC stakeholders might then seek to replace

---

[6] That is, screening for candidate dependability, reliability, conscientiousness, and other soft skills that could be indicative of overall trust.

traditional screening questions with new inquiries that focus on the types of metrics identified in suggestion 5.1.

Observation 6: Hiring flexibilities afforded to USG departments and agencies have proven beneficial during the course of the pandemic, but some are due to sunset after FY 2022. Use of digital signatures, video interviews (with candidates and their listed contacts), and other relaxed I-9 verification mechanisms have helped to ensure continuity of national security operations and staffing. For example, DHS physical-presence deferment guidance (I-9 hiring flexibilities) were due to sunset in FY 2023, while some Schedule A hiring authorities have been extended to March 2023.[7] We also note that many of the virtual practices used during the initial stages of the COVID-19 pandemic are already reverting to traditional in-person interviews, phone-calls, and hard-copy/paper-based security forms.

- **Suggestion 6.1.** The USG might consider developing a survey for investigative service providers across the SSC enterprise to help identify key "pain-points" for investigators and what specific technologies or processes helped achieve their investigative missions during the early stages of the pandemic.[8]
- **Suggestion 6.2.** The USG should also consider cataloging informal guidance developed by individual departments and agencies to identify cross-cutting challenges and enablers that could be rapidly operationalized to address hiring and screening in the event of a future global pandemic or other catastrophic event that would affect the USG's ability to rapidly hire and onboard a diverse national security workforce.

Conclusion

Global pandemic conditions have provided more impetus for continued modernization of SSC processes into the mobile realm. Pandemic operating conditions demonstrated the USG's national security resilience in maintaining an effective workforce but also revealed wide-ranging vulnerabilities across traditional SSC vetting processes.

Between the late 1990s and early 2000s, a flurry of federal hiring activities and authorities gave rise to automated hiring systems and created several hiring flexibilities (i.e., the Federal Career Intern Program [2000], direct hire and category rating [2002], and the Federal Workforce Flexibility Act [2004]) that are now common practice across USG entities.[9] Despite prolific use of video interviews and other virtual platforms during the pandemic to assist USG candidate

---

[7] For more on the authority extension for screening processes, see U.S. Citizenship and Immigration Service, 2022a. For more on the authority extension for Schedule A hiring processes, see Chief Human Capital Officers Council, "Extension of the Coronavirus COVID-19 Schedule A Hiring Authority," June 27, 2022.

[8] This is in line with Suggestion 1.2.

[9] U.S. Merit Systems Protection Board, *Reforming Federal Hiring*, report to the President and the Congress of the United States, undated.

screening efforts, many organizations appear reluctant to rely on AI, ML, or other algorithm-based platforms to safeguard against risks associated with national security information. While we do not suggest moving to a fully automated screening process (the SSC process must retain a "human-in-the-loop"), we do suggest that mobile technology can greatly enhance—and even replace—some outdated elements of the SSC process in line with TW 2.0 goals and objectives.

Mobile technology could offer several advantages over traditional screening processes. Mobile platforms could enable increased interaction with candidates entering the SSC process and those who may be interested in pursuing a career in national security. A USG-approved mobile application could reduce the need for travel, follow-up interviews, and other administrative errands, allowing investigators to shift their focus to ensuring that the USG will receive the right people for the right job. Mobile technology use could also improve USG retention practices by identifying career pathways that cater to candidate skills and interests, which could assist in mitigating hiring gaps during future periods of uncertainty.

However, even the most high-tech mobile device or application cannot fully replace human investigators or adjudicators. Investigators and adjudicators bring a wealth of empirical experience that is difficult (if not impossible) to replicate via software. Detecting anomalies within baseline data is useful for binary data collection, but mobile platforms cannot account for qualitative aspects of human experience required to assess whether an employee should have access to sensitive information.[10]

This exploratory research has identified several steps that the USG might consider as it seeks to modernize the SSC process. This research suggests that availability of technology is not the issue, but it is rather the institutional vetting culture that may present the largest obstacle to future mobile implementation. Future research in this area should explore some of the more sensitive underlying methods within the SSC process with investigators and adjudicators to identify key gaps or cross-cutting information gaps that cause delays in hiring. Identified gaps could then be aligned to supporting technologies. As our interviews revealed, it is not a matter of *if* a future event similar to the COVID-19 pandemic affects the SSC process, but *when*. An institutionalized mobile or virtual capability for SSC processes would help ensure an expedited and continuous flow of trusted USG employees and contractor support, serving as a critical safeguard amid a global state of uncertainty.

---

[10] That is, ML and AI cannot account for whole-of-person concepts dictated within investigative or adjudicative guidelines. However, mobile platforms could provide a set of indicators that would be further explored by human staff.

USG and Private-Sector Interview Protocols

Project Overview and HSPC Statement

Thank you for taking the time to speak with us today. We're from the RAND Corporation, a nonprofit, nonpartisan institution that conducts research on behalf of the U.S. government, private institutions, and foreign governments.

Our study is focused on assisting the U.S. Government's Performance Accountability Council Program Management Office (PAC PMO) with an examination of how organizational vetting processes and procedures can be enhanced by increasing interaction with individuals through mobile technologies and platforms. Our project will identify key mobile platform and security factors to consider when communicating with and screening candidates within the security clearance process and will also highlight relevant private sector practices on talent acquisition, ATS, screening methods, and communication strategies with candidates prior to the onboarding process.

We are seeking to 1) categorize emerging mobile technology platforms based on security, suitability, or credentialing (SSC) process relevance and ability to assist government vetting of personnel; 2) illustrate relevant practices and lessons learned for integrating security applications with mobile platforms; and 3) provide recommendations on how best to incorporate potentially useful private sector screening practices to create efficiency within initial stages of the hiring process.

Per RAND's Human Subjects Protection Committee guidance, we will be taking detailed notes during this interview, but your responses will be kept anonymous; we will not share our interview notes or your personal information outside our small project team. Your participation in this interview is voluntary and let us know if you would prefer not to answer any of the questions we pose.

If you have further questions about your rights as a research participant or need to report a research-related injury or concern, you can contact RAND's Human Subjects Protection Committee toll-free at (866) 697-5620 or by emailing hspcinfo@rand.org.

Do you have any questions before we begin?

USG Interview Protocol

Organizational Details

1. Can you tell us about your current role in your organization?
2. Can you estimate the general size of your organization?
3. Can you describe the type, or range of personnel your organization is seeking to hire? (e.g. analysts, IT support folks)
4. Are you able to discuss some of your current hiring priorities?
5. Does your organization tend to actively recruit potential candidates in person (e.g. at college campuses, job fairs, etc.) or is it mostly online based?
   a. Has COVID changed that mix (e.g. 60/40, 50/50)?
6. Does your organization distinguish hiring practices from onboarding practices? Where is the divide?

Risk Assessment

1. Can you discuss the types of risks that employees could present to your institution?
   a. Which risks are most potentially damaging to your institution?
2. Which types of employee roles present the greatest risk? Why?
3. Does your organization differentiate between vetting for trust and vetting for skills?

Risk Mitigation

1. What does your company do to detect, guard against, and mitigate risks during initial hiring phases?
   a. Are any of those activities conducted once onboarded (e.g. performance monitoring/detection of violations/termination)?
2. Who executes these functions and are those conducted in-house or contracted out?
3. Has your screening process changed in the last few years due to data leaks, new and emerging threats, or concerns for data privacy?
4. What role do interviews play in the overall vetting process?
5. How do you test candidate skills in this phase of hiring? (e.g. gaming, workshops, others?)

Specific Mobile/Platform Vetting Practices/Processes

1. Can you describe how (or if) your organization uses mobile or virtual screening methods during candidate outreach, or during initial hiring phases?
   a. Are technologies deployed during initial reach-out, interview-phases, other phases?

2.	Can you describe the current (or primary) virtual platforms you use when reaching out to candidates?

	a.	Was this hiring-method in place prior to COVID?

3.	Can you list of any vetting, screening, or monitoring platforms that you use?

4.	What are the key factors those programs look for/seeks to uncover?

5.	Are there any types of adjudication for platform results?

6.	Are there any other particularly innovative or notable approaches that your organization undertakes to expedite hiring and onboarding? If so, what are they?

7.	How/or do you inform candidates about the use of these technologies during screening?

8.	Do you incorporate mobile technology into retention practices (e.g., individuals updating Linked-in or Facebook information to reach-out to other firms)?

Platform Efficiency/Effectiveness

1.	Are there any major barriers to using this software/application? (e.g., cost, law/privacy considerations, integration interoperability with virtual platforms)

2.	Might you be able to provide examples of where the program effectively "weeded" someone out?

	a.	Any examples of the program providing a false reading (e.g., an indication or spike not indicative of candidate trust or reliability)

	a.	If so, how did your organization handle the false reading with the candidate?

3.	Do you have metrics for platform success? (e.g., use of platform/technology decreased hiring timeline by X, or saved us this much $, cost per hire assessment).

4.	What is the process for integrating platform results with the rest of the hiring process (i.e., how quick is the OODA loop?)

5.	What are the efficiencies gained through this method vs. traditional HR processes?

6.	Do you have any other procedures or technologies in place designed to reduce unqualified applications?

7.	Does your company or vendor also perform social media checks – and at what point in the hiring process does this occur?

Future Look

1.	What is the game-changing (or biggest) factor that will impact hiring and recruitment in the next 5 years? Next 10 years?

Closing

1.	Before we close the discussion, is there anything else you want to add or any other area we should be considering to help the government think about what they might do to "reimagine" how the IC does hiring and onboarding in an efficient and effective way?

2. Any questions that we haven't asked that we should have?
3. Can you recommend anyone else we should talk to in this space?

Private-Sector Interview Protocol

Organizational Details

1. Can you tell us about your current role in your organization?
2. Can you estimate the general size of your organization?
3. Can you describe the type, or range of personnel your organization is seeking to hire? (e.g. analysts, IT support folks)
4. Are you able to discuss some of your current hiring priorities?
5. Does your organization tend to actively recruit potential candidates in person (e.g. at college campuses, job fairs, etc.) or is it mostly online based?
    a. Has COVID changed that mix (e.g. 60/40, 50/50)
6. Does your organization distinguish hiring practices from onboarding practices? Where is the divide?

Risk Assessment

1. Can you discuss the types of risks that employees could present to your institution?
    a. Which risks are most potentially damaging to your institution?
2. Which types of employee roles present the greatest risk? Why?
3. Does your organization differentiate between vetting for trust and vetting for skills?

Risk Mitigation

1. What does your company do to detect, guard against, and mitigate these risks during initial hiring phases?
    a. Are any of those activities conducted once onboarded? (e.g. performance monitoring/detection of violations/termination)
2. Who executes these functions and are those conducted in-house or contracted out?
3. Has your screening process changed in the last few years due to data leaks, new and emerging threats, or concerns for data privacy?
4. What role do interviews play in the overall vetting process?
5. How do you test candidate skills in this phase of hiring? (e.g. gaming, workshops, others?)

Specific Mobile/Platform Vetting Practices/Processes

1. Can you describe how (or if) your organization uses mobile or virtual screening methods during candidate reach out, or during initial hiring phases?
   a. Are technologies deployed during initial reach-out, interview-phases, other phases?
2. Can you describe the current (or primary) virtual platforms you use when reaching out to candidates?
   a. Was this hiring-method in place prior to COVID?
3. Can you list of any of the vetting, screening, or monitoring platforms that you use?
4. What are the key factors those programs look for/seeks to uncover?
5. Are there any types of adjudication for platform results?
6. Are there any other particularly innovative or notable approaches that your organization undertakes to expedite hiring and onboarding? If so, what are they?
7. How/or do you inform candidates about the use of these technologies during screening?
8. Do you incorporate mobile technology into retention practices? (e.g., updating linkedin, Facebook reach-out to other firms)

Platform Efficiency/Effectiveness

1. Are there any major barriers to using this software/application? (e.g., cost, law/privacy considerations, integration interoperability with virtual platforms)
2. Might you be able to provide examples of where the program effectively "weeded" someone out?
   a. Any examples of the program providing a false reading (e.g. an indication or spike not indicative of candidate trust or reliability)
3. Do you have metrics for platform success? (e.g., use of platform/technology decreased hiring timeline by X, or saved us this much $, cost per hire assessment).
4. What is the process for integrating platform results with the rest of the hiring process (i.e., how quick is the OODA loop?)
5. What are the efficiencies gained through this method vs. traditional HR processes?
6. Do you have any other procedures or technologies in place designed to reduce unqualified applications?
7. Does your company or vendor also perform social media checks – and at what point in the hiring process does this occur?

Future Look

1. What is the game-changing (or biggest) factor that will impact hiring and recruitment in the next 5 years? Next 10 years?

Closing

1. Before we close the discussion, is there anything else you want to add or any other area we should be considering to help the government think about what they might do to "reimagine" how the IC does hiring and onboarding in an efficient and effective way?
2. Any questions that we haven't asked that we should have?
3. Can you recommend anyone else we should talk to in this space?

Annotated Bibliography for Chapter 2

This annotated bibliography highlights key practices, potential innovative approaches, and challenges, where applicable, from the public and private sectors and academic institutions. This annotated bibliography is not intended to be an exhaustive list of every source that might pertain to mobile PV, though it is intended to provide a selection of literature that the RAND team identified as the most relevant publicly available and unclassified sources. Table B.1. summarizes key findings from the literature review.

The annotated bibliography below is ordered chronologically from the oldest to newest sources.[1]

Peterson, Andrea, "Some Companies Are Tracking Workers with Smartphone Apps. What Could Possibly Go Wrong?" *Washington Post*, May 14, 2015.

- *Challenges:* Perception that employers do not trust their workforce (i.e., otherwise they wouldn't need to track their locations via mobile monitoring technologies). Ethical and legal challenges of monitoring employees while they are off duty and not allowing them to turn their mobile devices off—ever—or face termination. There are few, if any, policies and guidelines for when it is appropriate to track employees' physical location, and sensitive personal information can be pieced together from continuous monitoring.
- *Enablers:* Proliferation of mobile monitoring technologies (e.g., GPS monitoring, automatic time-tracking)
- *Best practices:* None mentioned.

Harwell, Drew, "Federal Study Confirms Racial Bias of Many Facial-Recognition Systems, Casts Doubt on Their Expanding Use," *Washington Post*, December 19, 2019.

- *Challenges:* Facial recognition systems misidentified people of color more often than white people. Asian and African American people were up to 100 times more likely to be misidentified than white men. Native Americans had the highest false-positive rate of all ethnicities. African American women were falsely identified more often by sys-

---

[1] By *enablers*, we mean factors that drive successful implementation of mobile technologies in the federal hiring and vetting process. By *challenges*, we mean factors that impede or otherwise create barriers to successful implementation of mobile technologies in the federal hiring and vetting process. *Best practices* are lessons learned from federal organizations—as well as employers in the private sector—that have aided the successful implementation of mobile technologies in the federal hiring and vetting process and provided ways to overcome challenges.

TABLE B.1

Findings from the Literature Review

Category	Findings
Challenges	• Perceptions of a lack of trust and the potential for discrimination, harassment, and workplace humiliation • Ethical, legal, and cybersecurity challenges related to the use of mobile technologies in hiring (e.g., embedded biases, sensitive personal data protection, inaccuracy) • Lack of policies and guidelines for the use of technology in federal hiring processes • The federal hiring and vetting process hasn't changed in a long time—getting agencies to let go of traditional elements of the hiring and vetting process (e.g., in-person interviews) is difficult, even though traditional federal hiring practices are often insufficient to meet demands for talent • Frequently changing, revising, and extending remote work policies over the course of the pandemic can lead to confusion as to when certain policies will sunset • It is difficult to collect information on how the federal hiring and vetting process is evolving in the digital environment • Many mandatory pre-employment activities take approximately 30 days to complete (e.g., physicals, drug tests, reference checks, credentialing) • DHS flexibilities apply only to employers operating entirely remotely • Many COVID-19 hiring and onboarding flexibilities are temporary and limited to the duration of the national health emergency • Schedule A hiring authority for federal agencies can be used only for COVID-19 response and not to fill any other organizational vacancy • Maintaining mobile hiring and vetting flexibilities afforded by the pandemic may require changes in legislation and regulations • Uptake of OPM's mobile hiring and assessment services has been slow • Options for federal agencies to bring in large numbers of qualified staff quickly exist (e.g., a 2016 GAO report found 105 hiring authorities) but are not widely known and are underused • Agencies must be able to predict their hiring levels at least a year out to take advantage of the OPM Presidential Management Fellows Program • Most of the hiring authorities (e.g., Schedule A, Title 38) that can expedite hiring are limited to the excepted service • Older employees may struggle to adapt to mobile hiring, vetting, and onboarding processes • Federal agency IT and digital infrastructure may not support robust hiring and vetting mobile technology implementation

Table B.1—Continued

Category	Findings
Enablers	• Proliferation of mobile monitoring technologies (e.g., GPS, automatic time tracking, facial recognition, AI and ML, digital sensors, high-quality webcams) • The pandemic fueled rapid adoption of mobile technologies for remote recruiting, hiring, onboarding, and employee monitoring • Benefits of mobile hiring and vetting technologies include streamlining the process, reducing the time-to-hire, cost-savings (e.g., reduction in travel expenses), increasing talent pool to include more racial/ethnic, gender, and geographically diverse candidates, process more candidates, and increase retention • OPM started offering VI and assessment services in 2019, advised federal agencies to virtually or remotely onboard new employees (including remote fingerprinting) during the COVID-19 pandemic, and authorized Schedule A hiring authority • GSA already had some digital infrastructure in place at the onset of the pandemic, which allowed it to transition to mobile hiring and vetting processes must more easily and faster • Noncompetitive hiring authorities enable agencies to make appointments without using Title 5 competitive examining procedures • OPM and Congress have the power to establish direct hiring authorities, which is another potential flexibility for agencies to use • OPM's Presidential Management Fellows program allows agencies to hire prequalified candidates for a two-year period in the excepted service, and agencies may convert fellows to permanent positions in the competitive service • VHA modified its careers website to enable candidates to start the hiring process directly with the agency in lieu of going through USAJobs, which cut down the time-to-hire from 94 days to a few weeks

Best practices	• The use of mobile technologies in the hiring, vetting, and onboarding processes—as well as continuous employee monitoring—requires transparency
	• Do not frame the use of mobile technologies in the hiring, vetting, onboarding, or continuous monitoring processes as a means of "bringing people together"—candidates and employees may perceive this as disingenuous
	• Employers have a responsibility to scrutinize any technology for bias and discrimination before implementation, and agencies should consider regularly auditing their mobile hiring and vetting technologies to ensure accuracy and security
	• Physical presence (i.e., in-person) is still considered best practice for identity and employment eligibility verification
	• Agency HR directors should work with their respective CIOs to determine the best ways forward to implement mobile technologies in the hiring and onboarding process
	• Ensure onboarding documents are available electronically
	• There are five critical elements to successful integration of mobile technologies in the hiring and vetting process:
	  a. Predictive validity
	  b. Transparency and candidate experience
	  c. Security, privacy, and records retention
	  d. Candidate pools and efficiency
	  e. Diversity
	• Federal agencies must shift their mindsets and understand that hiring is a business process and not a regulatory issue
	• Apply a project management approach to the hiring and vetting processes—HR teams should prioritize clear and frequent communication with candidates, as well as with hiring managers, SMEs, agency leaders, and other stakeholders
	• Federal agencies should develop a recruiting infrastructure by leveraging data and mobile technology and hiring recruiters or training staff on how to interact with candidates
	• Build relationships with IT and other support functions at both senior and staffing level

SOURCE: Summary of key findings from the RAND literature review conducted during this study and cited in this report.

tems used frequently by law enforcement. Such errors and misidentification can make it easier for imposters to gain access to critical systems. California and Massachusetts have banned use of facial recognition by public officials.

- *Enablers:* Proliferation in the use of facial recognition by law enforcement and government agencies. There is no national regulation or standard for facial recognition algorithms, and local law enforcement agencies rely on a wide range of contractors and systems with different capabilities and varying levels of accuracy.
- *Best practices:* Any company or government that deploys new technology has a responsibility to scrutinize the product for bias and discrimination at least as thoroughly as it would look for bugs in the software.

DHS, "ICE Announces Flexibility in Requirements Related to Form I-9 Compliance," March 23, 2020.

- *Challenges:* Employers must submit written documentation of their remote onboarding and telework policies for each employee. Once normal operations resume [and the extensions of this policy sunset], all employees onboarded remotely will have to report to their employer physically within three business days for in-person verification of identity and employment eligibility documentation.
- *Enablers:* Precautions being implemented by employers and employees related to physical proximity associated with COVID-19. DHS will exercise discretion to defer the physical presence requirements associated with Employment Eligibility Verification (Form I-9) under Section 274A of the Immigration and Nationality Act. Employers must inspect the Section 2 documents remotely (e.g., over video link, fax, email, etc.) and obtain, inspect, and retain copies of the documents within three business days.
- *Best practices:* Physical presence is best practice for identity and employment eligibility verification.

Ogrysko, Nicole, "Agencies Can Virtually Onboard New Employees During Coronavirus Pandemic," Federal News Network, March 24, 2020.

- *Challenges:* DHS flexibilities apply only to employers who are operating entirely remotely. All mobile and remote hiring and onboarding procedures implemented because of the COVID-19 pandemic are temporary and apply only to the length of the current national public health emergency. Federal agencies can use the Schedule A hiring authority only for COVID-19 response and cannot use it to fill any other organizational vacancy.
- *Enablers:* OPM advised agencies to virtually or remotely onboard new employees. DHS added some flexibilities to the employee eligibility verification requirements. OPM authorized Schedule A hiring authority for federal agencies.
- *Best practices:* Agency HR directors should work with their respective CIOs to determine the best ways forward and offer the oath of office to new employees over a video platform. Agencies should make onboarding documents available electronically, and new employees should be able to sign these documents and email them to their agen-

cies either with an electronic form and signature or by taking a picture of the completed document.

OPM, "Temporary Procedures for Personnel Vetting and Appointment of New Employees During Maximum Telework Period Due to COVID-19," Policy, Data, Oversight Memorandum, March 25, 2020.

- *Challenges:* Federal agencies experiencing challenges collecting fingerprints to meet existing requirements for a fingerprint check of the FBI's criminal history records as part of vetting new hires and contractors, appointments to the civil service, and determining eligibility for issuance of PIV credentials. The guidance states that "Remote inspections will be an interim process. . . ."
- *Enablers:* Many federal, state, and local offices that take fingerprints are temporarily closed due to measures associated with COVID-19. OPM's guidance permits continued onboarding when fingerprinting is not immediately available. The guidance states that "When agencies are unable to perform the identity proofing processes for determining eligibility and for issuance of a credential consistent with the agency head's determination of risk, they may elect instead to perform the identity proofing via remote inspection (e.g., over video link, fax or e-mail, etc.)."
- *Best practices:* Once an agency can collect fingerprints for an individual, the agency must submit them to the appropriate agency or office.

Harwell, Drew, "Managers Turn to Surveillance Software, Always-On Webcams to Ensure Employees Are (Really) Working from Home," *Washington Post*, April 30, 2020.

- *Challenges:* Some older employees may struggle to adapt to mobile hiring, vetting, and onboarding processes. Always-on webcam mandates, overscheduling virtual check-ins, and inundating employees with not-so-optional virtual events can increase stress, anxiety, exhaustion, and burnout. Employees feel use of these sorts of mobile monitoring technologies means their employer fundamentally distrusts them. Ethical and legal challenges have been associated with employers installing mobile monitoring software that creates a minute-by-minute timeline of every app and website viewed, keystrokes, and webcam images and categorizes these as either productive or unproductive—all without the employee's knowledge that they are being monitored so closely. People don't work well under that level of intense monitoring. Minute-by-minute photos open up possibilities of discrimination, harassment, and workplace humiliation—e.g., "the service allows anyone to instantly send a photo of their co-worker to an open Slack channel when an employee does something silly like pick their nose."
- *Enablers:* The COVID-19 pandemic incentivized employers to find ways to keep employees in line and on task by packing their social calendars with virtual events and tracking their productivity to ensure they are telling the truth about working from home. The "tattleware" industry caters to company leaders who want to peer over their employees' shoulders and confirm their productivity.

- *Best practices:* Transparency. Do not try to frame continuous mobile monitoring (e.g., always-on webcams and microphones, keystrokes, mouse activity, minute-by-minute screenshots and photos) as "bringing workers closer together."

Miller, Jason, "Online Interviews, Virtual Oaths of Office Are Some of the Ways Agencies Are Evolving Hiring," Federal News Network, May 11, 2020.

- *Challenges:* The hiring process hasn't changed in a long time, and there are still regulations in place that dictate the framework by which hiring is conducted. The federal hiring process is convoluted, difficult, and reduces the level of agility the federal government needs. One area that will become more stressed is the post-hiring decision point. The onboarding process includes provisioning employees with the assets they need, such as laptops and cellphones, email addresses, and access to the agency's network. Details on how the hiring process is evolving are hard to come by within the federal government. Post-OPM's memo urging agencies to adopt commercial best practices and use mobile technologies, uptake has still been slow. One thing agencies need is a robust technology platform that can handle high volumes of applications from thousands of locations at the same time. Another challenge is getting agencies to let go of traditional elements of the hiring process that don't add value and aren't reliant on any regulatory requirement.
- *Enablers:* GSA had much of the digital infrastructure already in place at the onset of the pandemic, which allowed it to transition to remote hiring, vetting, and onboarding relatively easily. Some agencies are showing that, if applied correctly, technology can improve the efficiency of the hiring effort, process more candidates, and enable more interviews. It also takes some of the burden of in-person interaction out of the picture. OPM reported that the time to hire an employee from first application to getting them fully onboarded was 98 days, which was down from 105.8 days in 2016 and 2017. OPM started offering VI and assessment services in 2019. Mobile technologies in the hiring and vetting process can lead to cutting the time to hire, improving the quality of candidates, and keeping the retention rate high. Virtual hiring fairs have been successful for decades and bring in more than 3,500 candidates annually. Current mobile technologies offer almost the same experience as in-person, so there is less and less reason for agencies to not take advantage of them.
- *Best practices:* GSA's experience and initial success can provide best practices and lessons learned for other organizations. There are five critical elements of successful integration of mobile technologies in the hiring and vetting process: (1) predictive validity; (2) transparency and candidate experience; (3) security, privacy, and records retention; (4) candidate pools and efficiency; and (5) diversity. Agencies need to shift their mindsets and understand that hiring is a business process and not a regulatory issue.

Friedman, Gary D., and Thomas McCarthy, "Employment Law Red Flags in the Use of Artificial Intelligence in Hiring," *Business Law Today*, October 1, 2020.

- *Challenges:* Prior to the pandemic, many businesses were already beginning to migrate toward the use of AI for screening applications—however, without proper vetting and analysis, these technologies can introduce bias into the process and expose employers to liability under various federal, state, and local laws. Technologies used in the hiring process are only as good as the programmers who developed them—and even in cases in which an algorithm is sound, if the data fed into it (e.g., previous hiring decisions) is not, then the output will continue to be biased. For example, an algorithm trained to prefer candidates within a certain commute radius might result in applicants from poorer areas being disadvantaged. If the technologies implemented in the hiring process result in certain groups being unfairly disadvantaged, then it opens employers to potential claims under various antidiscrimination laws, such as Title VII of the Civil Rights Act of 1964, the Age Discrimination in Employment Act, and the Americans with Disabilities Act. Moreover, certain biometric laws may apply when biometric identifiers (e.g., finger-prints) are collected, as those employers must specify how they safeguard, handle, store, and destroy the data they collect and provide individuals with prior notice and consent. Illinois has enacted a first-of-its-kind law—the Artificial Intelligence Video Interview Act—that imposes strict limits on employers who use AI to analyze candidate video interviews. New York is also considering legislation to limit discriminatory use of AI, which would prohibit the sale of automated employment decision tools unless the tools' developers first conducted antibias audits to assess the tools' predicted compliance with the provisions of Section 8-107 of the New York City Code. The Algorithmic Account-ability Act was introduced in April 2019; it is the first proposed federal law aimed at regulating the use of algorithms by private companies and would task the Federal Trade Commission with creating regulations that require employers to assess their AI tools for accuracy, fairness, bias, discrimination, privacy, and security.
- *Enablers:* During the COVID-19 pandemic, businesses have been forced to reassess their recruitment, hiring, vetting, and onboarding processes, including abandoning tradi-tional in-person interviews and job assessments in favor of virtual meetings and the use of online tools to measure, among other things, cognitive capabilities, emotional intelligence, personality traits, and skill sets. Utilizing technology in the screening and hiring process is not new—for several decades, simple text searches have been used to cull resumes. Now, AI is used to understand and compare experiences across resumes to determine which candidate more closely matches the requirements of a job posting. Once a candidate has been identified, AI chat bots can automatically reach out to initi-ate document requests and interview scheduling. Some companies are also using neu-roscientific computer games to assess and predict candidates' cognitive and personality traits.
- *Best practices:* Employers should consider auditing their mobile technologies used in the hiring and vetting process regularly. Utilizing contractors to either develop or use their

mobile technologies does not protect the employer from liability if the vendor is using tools that discriminate against protected groups, just as companies may be held liable for violations of employment laws by recruiting companies.

Partnership for Public Service, *Rapid Reinforcements: Strategies for Federal Surge Hiring,* **Democracy Fund, October 2020.**

- *Challenges:* Federal hiring practices are often insufficient to meet the immediate demands for additional talent. Ordinarily, the federal hiring process can take more than a year and lasts more than three months on average, which is more than twice the time it takes the private sector. Options are available for federal agencies to bring in large numbers of qualified staff quickly, though they are not widely known and are underused. The typical federal hiring process makes agencies less competitive with the private sector, as many candidates opt for private-sector positions that they can land faster instead of waiting months to become a government employee. Most of the hiring authorities (e.g., Schedule A, Title 38) that can expedite hiring are limited to the excepted service. Agencies tend to rely on traditional hiring authorities, and there is widespread unfamiliarity with the many options available; furthermore, some hiring authorities lack broad utility—for example, a 2016 GAO report found that only 20 of the 105 hiring authorities accounted for 91 percent of new hires that year. Budget limitations may prohibit hiring professional recruiters or adopting new technologies. The complexity of the federal hiring process slows it down. To take advantage of OPM's Presidential Management Fellows Program, agencies must be able to predict their hiring levels and submit data to OPM by July of each year, since there is a cap on the number of program finalists each year.
- *Enablers:* Within the competitive service, there are noncompetitive hiring authorities that enable agencies to make appointments without using Title 5 competitive examining procedures, thereby streamlining the process. Direct hiring authority is another flexibility within the competitive service that can accelerate hiring because it does not require an application of veterans' preferences or applicant rating and ranking. Both Congress and OPM have the power to establish direct hiring authorities. Examples of government-wise direct hiring authorities include those for certain cybersecurity; science, technology, engineering, and math (STEM); and medical positions, but OPM may grant them to specific agencies for certain occupational series, pay grades, or geographic locations in response to an urgent need. The Department of Health and Human Services created HR Exchange, which is a customer-centric online platform for modernizing HR service delivery. OPM's Presidential Management Fellows Program facilitates a process whereby agencies can hire prequalified candidates for a two-year paid position in the excepted service, and agencies may convert fellows to permanent positions in the competitive services.
- *Best practices:* Agencies should ensure that their hiring practices—including those beyond the standard federal processes—are transparent and conducive to appropriate

oversight. Agencies must remain faithful to the federal merit system. Develop recruiting infrastructure by leveraging data and technology and by hiring recruiters or training current staff on how to attract candidates and guide them through the hiring process. Apply a project management approach to streamlining the hiring process, which means HR teams should prioritize clear and frequent communication with candidates, as well as with hiring managers, SMEs, agency leaders, and other stakeholders. For example, GSA's Technology Transformation Services use project management software to visualize candidate progress in each of its hiring actions. GSA has developed a hiring methods chart to facilitate strategic decisions about using hiring authorities.

Hayes, Heather B., "Virtual Tools Allow Agencies to Onboard New Workers from a Distance," *FedTech Magazine*, February 19, 2021.

- *Challenges:* COVID-19 shutdowns forced agencies to hire and onboard people virtually—and not all agencies were prepared to shift HR online. Onboarding in a short time frame is difficult, considering that the many mandatory preemployment activities, such as physicals, drug testing, reference checks, and credentialing, usually take around 30 days. Agencies had to balance risk and speed to make sure they were doing the appropriate amount of vetting for providers and eliminating potential red flags. Maintaining the flexibility afforded by pandemic hiring policies may require changes in legislation and regulations.
- *Enablers:* After the initial shock of mandated telework at the beginning of the pandemic wore off, HR functions continued normal operations. GSA repurposed digital tools the agency was already using internally for external HR functions. As a result, between March and September 2020, GSA interviewed more than 4,500 candidates and hired 572 employees. The pandemic and virtual work helped GSA accelerate innovation and employment. OPM had already set up an online onboarding capability for agencies' immediate use during the pandemic and granted permission to use virtual platforms to conduct legal tasks, such as administering oaths of office over video. The VHA and DHS took advantage of some of these newly established tools and policies. Mobile hiring technologies proved to be cost- and time-efficient. Jobs may become more location-agnostic, which will enable the federal government to cast a wider net for employees. VHA modified its VA Careers website (e.g., text-to-recruit app) to enable candidates to start the hiring process directly with VHA instead of having to go through USAJobs, which cut down the time to hire from 94 days to just a few weeks.
- *Best practices:* GSA virtualized and synchronized its national standardized onboarding program so its HR team could onboard new employees simultaneously, making the effort more efficient. Build relationships with IT and other support functions at both the senior and staffing level.

Cummings, Madeleine, "Screened out by a Computer? What Job Interviews Are Like Without Human Beings," CBC Radio, March 7, 2021.

- *Challenges:* As the pandemic continues, job seekers expect to attend employment interviews online, but, increasingly, employers and recruiters looking to hire are not attending virtual interviews in real time (i.e., asynchronous video interviews). However, some candidates find asynchronous video interviews uncomfortable, and some experts pose questions about fairness, privacy, bias, and the use of AI. Candidates feel that asynchronous video interviews are impersonal, they experience more anxiety by not talking to a person, and the format is unforgiving. Some candidates will not complete asynchronous video interviews out of their dislike of the format. There's a perception that, while it may be more efficient for employers, it signals to candidates that the agency is not invested in spending time to speak with candidates directly. Because many mobile hiring technology companies' algorithms are proprietary and not shared publicly, neither candidates nor academics can fully understand how the recorded interviews are evaluated. AI has the biases of its programmers built into it.
- *Enablers:* Asynchronous video interviews can eliminate the need for such logistics as scheduling interviews because candidates interview with the automated system at home on their own timeline. Asynchronous video interviews can also cut travel costs if candidates are screened out before having to meet a potential employer in person. Timed questions also force candidates to be more succinct with their answers than they might be in traditional interviews. Another reason hiring managers like asynchronous video interviews is that it allows employers to rewatch interviews and share them with colleagues.
- *Best practices:* Preparation for asynchronous video interviews should be a mandatory part of the curriculum at universities.

Partnership for Public Service, "Fed Figures: COVID-19 and the Federal Workforce," March 9, 2021.

- *Challenges:* The federal hiring process is insufficient in times of crisis when hiring demands surge.
- *Enablers:* Between March and December 2020, 15 Cabinet departments saw the average sizes of their workforces increase each quarter. During this time, the Federal Emergency Management Agency (FEMA) saw the largest expansion (an average 1.3 percent per quarter), while the National Institutes of Health (NIH) workforce retracted by 2.7 percent on average. VHA's national recruiting effort leveraged social media and other resources to attract candidates for many types of positions. VHA applicants interested in temporary appointments were encouraged to apply directly on the VHA website. The Small Business Administration used multiple hiring authorities, including Military Spouse Non-Competitive Appointing Authority, Returned Peace Corps Volunteer Non-Competitive Eligibility, and direct hire authorities to onboard more than 6,000 employees in six months.

- *Best practices:* VHA reduce the credentialing process from 30 days to three days, used data to resolve process inefficiencies, and staggered the onboarding process.

Accenture, "Going Virtual: How Federal Agencies Are Embracing the Hybrid Workforce," *Government Executive*, March 22, 2021.

- *Challenges:* When the pandemic began, onboarding trainings completely stopped in some agencies because they did not have policies or technologies in place to facilitate the process virtually. One challenge of using mobile technologies in hiring and vetting is that an interviewer may miss out on a little bit of body language, though they can still get a very good read on the candidate. It takes the federal government around 100 days for every hire, whereas it only takes an average of 45 days in the private sector. Challenges arise when an agency's policy has not caught up with the realities of the shift to remote work.

- *Enablers:* The U.S. Citizenship and Immigration Service (USCIS) worked with GSA to drastically reduce its physical facility presence, with an estimated savings of tens of millions of dollars annually per site. Federal agencies are learning that some virtual processes are more efficient than traditional in-person requirements. Virtual interviewing allows for people to be considered for a job regardless of their geographical location, which increases candidate pools and lowers interviewing costs, since the agency no longer had to pay for a candidate's travel and lodging. Candidates can complete assessments online, which is an advantage to HR managers—online assessments can help identify the candidates that align most closely with an agency's needs, competencies, and position requirements. Job position notices for remote jobs result in a much larger talent pipeline and a significant uptick in the number of applications received; emerging technologies can help agencies identify top candidates quickly. The ability to swiftly implement new policies while leveraging technology is critical to enabling a remote government workforce and can also have positive effects on diversity, equity, and inclusion programs.

- *Best practices:* Agencies need to adopt modern HR approaches that prioritize the candidate and employee experience by building on proven commercial best practices and harnessing the possibilities of new tools and technologies. Agencies need to embrace remote work by formalizing temporary policies that proved effective and efficient for their business and desirable to their employees. For example, USCIS acted quickly to rethink existing telework policy and developed a path to fully remote employment for most positions, which eliminated geographical ties to brick-and-mortar worksites. Remove obstacles in the application process to open the aperture to more qualified candidates and put the necessary tools in place so as to avoid overwhelming the system. Implementing technology that makes data more readily available and having a strategy for how to make that data actionable for key leaders empowers better and faster decisionmaking in the hiring process. Change management practices are required to implement new mobile technologies and digital tools in the federal hiring process.

Vincent, James, "Amazon Delivery Drivers Have to Consent to Surveillance in Their Vans or Lose Their Jobs," *The Verge,* **March 24, 2021.**

- *Challenges:* It is difficult to determine exactly what kind of information is being collected because of the varying capabilities of different digital sensors and ML tools. The cameras Amazon is installing in its delivery vans record 100 percent of the time. AI is just as fallible as the humans that programmed it. Drivers perceive the use of cameras that are always recording as an invasion of privacy and micromanagement tool. Some drivers refused to sign the consent form and quit their jobs.
- *Enablers:* The ML-powered cameras are intended to identify dangerous behavior, such as whether the driver is yawning or checking their phone while driving, and can provide real-time feedback, such as telling a driver to take a break or keep their eyes on the road.
- *Best practices:* Amazon requires drivers in the United States to sign biometric (e.g., photographs, physical location, fingerprints) consent forms, since the company is using digital sensors and ML-powered cameras to monitor its delivery drivers to increase efficiency.

Hunter, Tatum, "Here Are All the Ways Your Boss Can Legally Monitor You," *Washington Post,* **August 20, 2021.**

- *Challenges:* There is nothing in one mobile monitoring company's privacy policy that prevents employers from disciplining employees who complain about a boss in an email to a coworker—or for misusing the tool in any way. The company stated that it cannot implement safeguards that prevent misuse of their technology without significantly hindering the software's capability. Members of the household are not necessarily immune to employee monitoring, even though they do not work at the employee's company. For example, these technologies can collect data from the microphone and speakers on a computer—which could record ambient noise from a home office. Surveillance makes employees lose trust and motivation.
- *Enablers:* On work-issued devices, employers can gather data from your keyboard, such as how often you're typing, and even your webcam, if it's in your employment agreement. On corporate internet connections, employers can likely see which sites you visit and can access emails sent from company accounts. Almost all types of employee monitoring are entirely legal, and, in general, employees have very limited options for recourse and little to no expectation of employee privacy. U.S. law allows companies to monitor employee communication that is part of the "normal course" of employment.
- *Best Practices:* Some states, such as Delaware and Connecticut, require employers provide written notice to employees if their electronic activity is being monitored. Be transparent about digital monitoring—the line between monitoring and surveillance depends on whether individual employees can opt out of data collection.

Abril, Danielle, and Drew Harwell, "Keystroke Tracking, Screenshots, and Facial Recognition: The Boss May Be Watching Long After the Pandemic," *Washington Post*, **September 24, 2021.**

- *Challenges:* Continuous, constant monitoring of employees working remotely via digital monitoring technologies like facial recognition and AI can add additional stress and anxiety to the workday. In some cases, it can also take time out of the workday when an employee must scan their face from three separate angles to be back into the system after looking away for too many seconds or shifting in their chair. "Knowing you're on camera all day long adds unnecessary nerve-wracking stress." There are ethical, legal, and security concerns when employers monitor their employees without their knowledge, and workers have little power to control how and when they are being monitored. Many algorithms have been shown to perform worse with people of color, which leaves employees of color worried that they could be penalized because of the color of their skin.

- *Enablers:* The COVID-19 pandemic fueled a rise in the use of mobile surveillance technologies by employers, which coincides with companies' use of more-traditional monitoring software that can track an employee's computer keystrokes, take screenshots, and, in some cases, record audio or video while they are working from home. Legally, employers have the upper hand when it comes to monitoring. "If it's a company device, you have zero expectation of privacy. . . . If it's a personal device, as long as there are clear policies in place in favor of monitoring for work purposes, the law is going to permit it."

- *Best Practices:* Be transparent and up front about the nature, scope, and type of monitoring that candidates will undergo during the hiring, vetting, and onboarding process. Privacy is an important part of the employer-employee relationship, and, ultimately, the goal is to foster a culture of collaboration and mutual trust. If employees are not given the full details of when and how they are monitored, and if they do not feel trusted at work, then they are more likely to refuse monitoring of any kind regardless of the purpose.

Harwell, Drew, "Contract Lawyers Face a Growing Invasion of Surveillance Programs That Monitor Their Work," *Washington Post*, **November 11, 2021.**

- *Challenges:* Facial recognition can have biases embedded, making it difficult for it to recognize the faces of people of color. Another example of embedded biases in employee monitoring software is mistaking the Bantu knots hairstyle as unauthorized recording devices. Such failures in facial recognition can add another stress and time to the workday—for instance, one contract lawyer was forced to log back in and rescan her face from three angles upward of 25 times a day. "The cost of all the heavy-handedness [of workplace monitoring] comes down on the employee." Employee monitoring technologies can be prone to error and imprecise, which allows for wild swings in accuracy depending on factors such as room lighting, a person's skin color, eyeglasses, hairstyle, or quality of the webcam. These technologies can lead to chastisement for harmless behaviors like holding a coffee mug (which the system can mistake for an authorized camera) or listening to a podcast on their personal phone. Employees worry that their performance and potential future employability could be negatively affected by the results of error-prone technologies. There are legal and ethical complexities tied to using monitoring technologies that claim to track demeanor and productivity and use these data to assign workers productivity scores that are used in company decisionmaking. "The number of false positives make it more of a nuisance than it's worth."

- *Enablers:* Schedule flexibility and outsourced contracts have opened more opportunities for work in the saturated legal profession. "The pandemic pushed many of them out of secure document-review offices and into remote work, and many expected some additional security, since they look at sensitive files for legal cases with strict confidentiality rules." There is employee monitoring software that uses webcams to record facial movements and surroundings and will send an alert if the employee takes photos of confidential documents, stops paying attention to the screen, or allows unauthorized individuals to enter the room. Colleges are increasingly using online proctoring technologies to monitoring students during exams. Other "on demand monitoring" software can track workers' idle and active time, record their screens and web browser history, patrol their background noise for unauthorized music or phone calls, and use the webcam to scan a worker's face or room for rule-breaking activity, such as eating or drinking or suspicious expressions, gestures, or behavior that might indicate whether anyone else may be near the computer screen.
- *Best Practices:* None mentioned.

Maurer, Roy, "With Virtual Interviews Here to Stay, Best Practices Are Needed," Society for Human Resource Management, November 15, 2021.

- *Challenges:* Many recruiters still consider in-person interviews the gold standard for both the candidate and the employer; however, this perception is changing, albeit slowly. "In person I can see body language better and am more likely to have a better experience with someone. Over video, it may not be bad, but I don't think it will ever be superior." For some employers, it may not be economically feasible to shift to a remote environment.
- *Enablers:* The use of videoconferencing technology for virtual job interviews exploded during the pandemic. A poll of 1,100 U.S. employers found that 82 percent of respondents adopted virtual interviews for candidates because of the pandemic, and 93 percent expect to continue using virtual interviews in the future. In a hybrid work environment, employers desire the ability to hold both remote and in-person interviews, and it also allows them to expand their hiring pools. There are multiple benefits to virtual interviews, including shortening the time to hire, streamlining the hiring process, and creating a better candidate experience. The pandemic particularly accelerated the use of asynchronous interviewing, in which candidates record their responses to predetermined interview questions and employers review these recordings at a separate time.

While in-person interactions may be more desirable, VI provides flexibility, cost savings, and collaboration.

- *Best Practices:* Ensure multiple hiring team members evaluate asynchronous video interviews so the decision on whether a candidate advances in the process is not solely dependent on one person, which can help reduce bias. Consider candidate preference when it comes to whether they participate in a video or in-person interview process.

U.S. Chief Information Officers Council, "CIO Council Priorities: The President's Management Agenda (PMA)," undated.

- *Challenges:* None mentioned.
- *Enablers:* Modernizing the federal government may improve the ability of agencies to deliver mission outcomes, provide excellent service, and effectively steward taxpayer dollars. Cross-Agency Priority (CAP) Goals are a tool used by leadership to accelerate Presidential priority programs in which implementation requires active collaboration among multiple agencies. One of the CAP goals is to modernize IT to increase productivity and security, which includes leveraging data as a strategic asset.
- *Best Practices:* None mentioned.

Abbreviations

AI	artificial intelligence
APA	Administrative Procedure Act
API	application programming interface
ATS	applicant tracking systems
CBP	Customs and Border Protection
CFR	Code of Federal Regulations
CHRI	criminal history record information
CIO	chief information officer
COVID-19	coronavirus disease 2019
CRM	customer relationship management
CRS	Congressional Research Service
CV	continuous vetting
CVR	Commercial Virtual Remote
DCSA	Defense Counterintelligence and Security Agency
DEIA	diversity, equity, inclusion, and access
DHS	U.S. Department of Homeland Security
DISA	Defense Information Systems Agency
DoD	U.S. Department of Defense
ECPA	Electronic Communications Privacy Act
ELSI	ethical, legal, and security implications
EO	executive order
e-QIP	Electronic Questionnaires for Investigations Processing
FBI	Federal Bureau of Investigation
FIPS	federal information processing standard

FISMA	Federal Information Security Management Act
FY	fiscal year
GAO	U.S. Government Accountability Office
GPS	global positioning system
GSA	U.S. General Services Administration
HIPAA	Health Insurance Portability and Accountability Act
HR	human resources
IC	intelligence community
ICE	DHS Immigration and Customs Enforcement
I/O	industrial organization
IP	intellectual property
IT	information technology
KSA	knowledge, skills, abilities
ML	machine learning
MOSAIC	Multipurpose Occupational Systems Analysis Inventory–Close-Ended
NDAA	National Defense Authorization Act
NIST	National Institute for Standards and Technology
ODNI	Office of the Director of National Intelligence
OPM	Office of Personnel Management
PAC	performance accountability council
PDT	Position Designation Tool
PII	personally identifiable information
PIV	Personal Identity Verification
PMO	Program Management Office
PR	periodic reinvestigation
PV	personnel vetting

RPA	Request for Personnel Action
SEAD	Security Executive Agency Directive
SES	Senior Executive Service
SF	Standard Form
SME	subject-matter expert
SMS	short message service
SSC	security, suitability, and credentialing
STIG	Security Technical Implementation Guides
SuitEA	Suitability Executive Agent
TW	Trusted Workforce
U.S.C.	U.S. Code
USCIS	U.S. Citizenship and Immigration Service
USG	U.S. government
USPS	U.S. Postal Service
VHA	U.S. Veterans Health Administration
VI	video interviewing

References

Abril, Danielle, and Drew Harwell, "Keystroke Tracking, Screenshots, and Facial Recognition: The Boss May Be Watching Long After the Pandemic," *Washington Post*, September 24, 2021. As of May 16, 2022:
https://www.washingtonpost.com/technology/2021/09/24/
remote-work-from-home-surveillance/

Accenture, "Going Virtual: How Federal Agencies Are Embracing the Hybrid Workforce," *Government Executive*, March 22, 2021. As of May 16, 2022:
https://www.govexec.com/sponsors/federal-innovator/2021/03/
going-virtual-how-federal-agencies-are-embracing-hybrid-workforce/172660/

Aigner, Dennis J., and Glen G. Cain, "Statistical Theories of Discrimination in Labor Markets," *ILR Review*, Vol. 30, No. 2, January 1977.

Barnett, Jackson, "Survey Finds DOD Contractors Know Little About Forthcoming Cyber Standards," *FEDSCOOP*, January 23, 2020. As of November 9, 2022:
https://www.fedscoop.com/defense-contractor-cmmc-cybersecurity-survey/

Biden, Joseph R., Jr., Executive Order 14035, "Executive Order on Diversity, Equity, Inclusion, and Accessibility in the Federal Workforce," June 25, 2021. As of November 14, 2022:
https://www.whitehouse.gov/briefing-room/presidential-actions/2021/06/25/
executive-order-on-diversity-equity-inclusion-and-accessibility-in-the-federal-workforce/

Bock, Laszlo, *Work Rules! Insights from Inside Google That Will Transform How You Live and Lead*, Twelve, 2015.

Boudreaux, Benjamin, Matthew A. DeNardo, Sarah W. Denton, Ricardo Sanchez, Katie Feistel, and Hardika Dayalani, *Data Privacy During Pandemics: A Scorecard Approach for Evaluating the Privacy Implications of COVID-19 Mobile Phone Surveillance Programs*, RAND Corporation, RR-A365-1, 2020. As of June 22, 2022:
https://www.rand.org/pubs/research_reports/RRA365-1.html

Brown, Ryan Andrew, Douglas Yeung, Diana Gehlhaus, and Kathryn O'Connor, *Corporate Knowledge for Government Decisionmakers Insights on Screening, Vetting, and Monitoring Processes*, RR-A275-1, RAND Corporation, 2020. As of November 9, 2022:
https://www.rand.org/pubs/research_reports/RRA275-1.html

Bush, George W., Executive Order 13467, "Reforming Processes Related to Suitability for Government Employment, Fitness for Contractor Employees, and Eligibility for Access to Classified National Security Information," June 30, 2008. As of November 9, 2022:
https://www.govinfo.gov/content/pkg/WCPD-2008-07-07/pdf/WCPD-2008-07-07-Pg932.pdf

CFR—*See* Code of Federal Regulations.

Chief Human Capital Officers Council, "Extension of the Coronavirus COVID-19 Schedule A Hiring Authority," June 27, 2022. As of November 9, 2022:
https://www.chcoc.gov/content/extension-coronavirus-covid-19-schedule-hiring-authority-1

Clinton, William J., Executive Order 12968, "Access to Classified Information," August 2, 1995. As of November 9, 2022:
https://www.govinfo.gov/content/pkg/FR-1995-08-07/pdf/95-19654.pdf

Constitution of the United States, National Archives, 1787.

Cummings, Madeleine, "Screened Out by a Computer? What Job Interviews Are Like Without Human Beings," CBC Radio, March 7, 2021. As of November 9, 2022:
https://www.cbc.ca/radio/costofliving/shut-up-and-take-our-money-can-canadians-actually-afford-to-start-spending-once-covid-is-under-control-1.5938032/
screened-out-by-a-computer-what-job-interviews-are-like-without-human-beings-1.5938098

DCSA—See Defense Counterintelligence and Security Agency.

Defense Counterintelligence and Security Agency, "Background Investigations," webpage, undated-a. As of August 8, 2022:
https://www.dcsa.mil/mc/pv/investigations/

Defense Counterintelligence and Security Agency, "Trusted Workforce 2.0 and Continuous Vetting," undated-b. As of November 9, 2022:
https://www.dcsa.mil/mc/pv/cv/

Defense Counterintelligence and Security Agency, "DCSA Enrolls U.S. Security Clearance Holders in Continuous Vetting Program," press release, October 1, 2021. As of November 9, 2022:
https://www.dcsa.mil/Portals/91/Documents/news/DCSA_Press%20Release%20Continuous%20Vetting_100121.pdf

Defense Counterintelligence and Security Agency, "Trusted Workforce 2.0: The Future of Personnel Vetting," *CDSE Pulse*, Vol. 2, No. 7, July 2021. As of November 9, 2022:
https://www.dcsa.mil/Portals/91/Documents/about/err/CDSE_Pulse_July2021.pdf

DHS—See U.S. Department of Homeland Security.

Donovan, Shaun, "Improving Administrative Functions Through Shared Services," Office of Management and Budget, Memorandum M-16-11, May 4, 2016. As of November 9, 2022:
https://obamawhitehouse.archives.gov/sites/default/files/omb/memoranda/2016/m-16-11.pdf

Dunbar, Brian, "Statement for the Record for Brian Dunbar, Assistant Director, Special Security Directorate, National Counterintelligence and Security Center," testimony before the Senate Select Committee on Intelligence Hearing on Security Clearance Reform, March 7, 2018.

Duster, Troy, "Introduction to Unconscious Racism Debate," *Social Psychology Quarterly*, Vol. 71, No. 1, 2008.

Etherington, Darrell, "LinkedIn Battens Down the Hatches on API Use, Limiting Full Access to Partners," *TechCrunch*, February 12, 2015. As of November 9, 2022:
https://techcrunch.com/2015/02/12/linkedin-battens-down-the-hatches-on-api-use-limiting-full-access-to-partners/

Friedman, Gary D., and Thomas McCarthy, "Employment Law Red Flags in the Use of Artificial Intelligence in Hiring," *Business Law Today*, October 1, 2020. As of November 9, 2022:
https://www.americanbar.org/groups/business_law/publications/blt/2020/10/ai-in-hiring/

GAO—*See* U.S. Government Accountability Office.

GSA—*See* U.S. General Services Administration,

Hakamaa, Marko, "Understanding Your Position Designation Determination," Clearance Jobs, November 23, 2013. As of June 15, 2022:
https://news.clearancejobs.com/2013/11/23/understanding-position-designation-determination/

Harwell, Drew, "Federal Study Confirms Racial Bias of Many Facial-Recognition Systems, Casts Doubt on Their Expanding Use," *Washington Post*, December 19, 2019. As of May 16, 2022:
https://www.washingtonpost.com/technology/2019/12/19/federal-study-confirms-racial-bias-many-facial-recognition-systems-casts-doubt-their-expanding-use/

Harwell, Drew, "Managers Turn to Surveillance Software, Always-On Webcams to Ensure Employees Are (Really) Working from Home," *Washington Post*, April 30, 2020. As of May 16, 2022:
https://www.washingtonpost.com/technology/2020/04/30/work-from-home-surveillance/

Harwell, Drew, "Contract Lawyers Face a Growing Invasion of Surveillance Programs That Monitor Their Work," *Washington Post*, November 11, 2021. As of May 16, 2022:
https://www.washingtonpost.com/technology/2021/11/11/lawyer-facial-recognition-monitoring/

Hayes, Heather B., "Virtual Tools Allow Agencies to Onboard New Workers from a Distance," *FedTech Magazine*, February 19, 2021. As of May 16, 2022:
https://fedtechmagazine.com/article/2021/02/
virtual-tools-allow-agencies-onboard-new-workers-distance

Heckman, Jory, "USPS Biometrics Program Leans on Its Biggest Asset: A Post Office in Every Neighborhood," Federal News Network, January 12, 2021. As of June 9, 2022:
https://federalnewsnetwork.com/big-data/2021/01/
usps-biometrics-program-leans-on-its-biggest-asset-a-post-office-in-every-neighborhood/

Hunter, Tatum, "Here Are All the Ways Your Boss Can Legally Monitor You," *Washington Post*, September 24, 2021. As of May 16, 2022:
https://www.washingtonpost.com/technology/2021/08/20/
work-from-home-computer-monitoring/

Illinois Compiled Statutes, 820 ILCS 42, Artificial Intelligence Video Interview Act, January 1, 2020.

Jurkowski, Stephanie, "Electronic Surveillance," webpage, Cornell Law School Legal Information Institute, July 2017. As of June 17, 2022:
https://www.law.cornell.edu/wex/electronic_surveillance

Kairys, David, "Unconscious Racism," *Temple Law Review*, Vol. 83, No. 4, 2011.

Klosowski, Thorin, "The State of Consumer Data Privacy Laws in the US (and Why It Matters)," *New York Times*, September 6, 2021. As of November 9, 2022:
https://www.nytimes.com/wirecutter/blog/state-of-privacy-laws-in-us/

Maurer, Roy, "With Virtual Interviews Here to Stay, Best Practices Are Needed," Society for Human Resource Management, November 15, 2021. As of May 16, 2022:
https://www.shrm.org/resourcesandtools/hr-topics/talent-acquisition/pages/virtual-video-interviews-best-practices-are-needed.aspx

Miller, Jason, "Online Interviews, Virtual Oaths of Office Are Some of the Ways Agencies Are Evolving Hiring," Federal News Network, May 11, 2020. As of May 13, 2022:
https://federalnewsnetwork.com/reporters-notebook-jason-miller/2020/05/
online-interviews-virtual-oaths-of-office-are-some-of-the-ways-agencies-are-evolving-hiring/

Mulvaney, Mick, "Comprehensive Plan for Reforming the Federal Government and Reducing the Federal Civilian Workforce," Office of Management and Budget, Memorandum M-17-22, April 12, 2017. As of November 9, 2022:
https://www.whitehouse.gov/wp-content/uploads/legacy_drupal_files/omb/
memoranda/2017/M-17-22.pdf

National Institute for Standards and Technology, "Vetting the Security of Mobile Applications," SP 800-163, Revision 1, April 19, 2019a. As of November 9, 2022:
https://www.nist.gov/news-events/news/2019/04/
vetting-security-mobile-applications-nist-publishes-sp-800-163-revision-1

National Institute for Standards and Technology, "Compliance FAQs: Federal Information Processing Standards (FIPS)," webpage, November 15, 2019b. As of January 20, 2023: https://www.nist.gov/standardsgov/compliance-faqs-federal-information-processing-standards-fips

National Institute for Standards and Technology, "Personal Identity Verification (PIV) of Federal Employees and Contractors," FIPS 201-3, January 2022. As of November 9, 2022: https://csrc.nist.gov/publications/detail/fips/201/3/final

NIST—*See* National Institute for Standards and Technology.

ODNI—*See* Office of the Director of National Intelligence.

Office of the Director of National Intelligence, "Security Executive Agent Directive 5: Collection, Use, and Retention of Publicly Available Social Media Information in Personnel Security Background Investigations and Adjudications," May 12, 2016.

Office of the Director of National Intelligence, "Security Executive Agent Directive 4: National Security Adjudicative Guidelines," June 8, 2017. As of November 9, 2022; https://www.dni.gov/files/NCSC/documents/Regulations/SEAD-4-Adjudicative-Guidelines-U.pdf

Office of the Director of National Intelligence, "Security Executive Agent Directive 6: Continuous Evaluation," January 12, 2018. As of November 9, 2022: https://www.dni.gov/files/NCSC/documents/Regulations/SEAD-6-continuous%20evaluation-U.pdf

Office of the Director of National Intelligence, National Counterintelligence and Security Center, "Security vs Suitability," webpage, undated. As of June 15, 2022: https://www.dni.gov/index.php/ncsc-how-we-work/ncsc-security-executive-agent/ncsc-reform/ncsc-security-clearance-reform

Office of the Director of National Intelligence and the Office of Personnel Management, "Federal Personnel Vetting Guidelines," February 10, 2022. As of November 9, 2022: https://www.dni.gov/files/NCSC/documents/Regulations/Federal_Personnel_Vetting_Guidelines_10FEB2022-15Jul22.pdf

Office of Personnel Management, "Forms," webpage, undated-a. As of June 15, 2022: https://www.opm.gov/forms/federal-investigation-forms

Office of Personnel Management, "Hybrid Work Environment Toolkit," toolkit, undated-b. As of June 8, 2022: https://www.opm.gov/policy-data-oversight/future-of-work/hybrid-work-environment-toolkit/

Office of Personnel Management, "Policy, Data, Oversight: Hiring Information," undated-c. As of February 8, 2022: https://www.opm.gov/policy-data-oversight/hiring-information/hiring-authorities/

Office of Personnel Management, "Policy, Data, Oversight: Human Capital Management, Hiring Process Analysis Tool," webpage, undated-d. As of November 9, 2022: https://www.opm.gov/policy-data-oversight/human-capital-management/hiring-reform/hiring-process-analysis-tool/

Office of Personnel Management, "Policy, Data, Oversight: OPM's MOSAIC Studies and Competencies," undated-e. As of November 9, 2022: https://www.opm.gov/policy-data-oversight/assessment-and-selection/competencies/

Office of Personnel Management, "Suitability Executive Agent: Suitability Adjudications," webpage, undated-f. As of August 2, 2022:
https://www.opm.gov/suitability/suitability-executive-agent/suitability-adjudications/

Office of Personnel Management, "Request for Personnel Action," Standard Form 52, Rev. 7/91, U.S. Office of Personnel Management FPM Supp. 296-33, July 1991. As of November 9, 2022:
https://www.va.gov/vaforms/va/pdf/sf52.pdf

Office of Personnel Management, "Position Designation Tool," September 2017a. As of November 9, 2022:
https://www.opm.gov/suitability/suitability-executive-agent/position-designation-tool/position-designation-system-with-glossary-2017.pdf

Office of Personnel Management, "Questionnaire for Public Trust Positions," December 2017b. As of November 9, 2022:
https://www.opm.gov/forms/pdf_fill/sf85p.pdf

Office of Personnel Management, "On-Boarding Processes for New Employees During the COVID-19 Emergency," memorandum, March 24, 2020. As of May 13, 2022:
https://www.chcoc.gov/content/boarding-processes-new-employees-during-covid-19-emergency

Office of Personnel Management, "Dual Compensation Waiver Requests for COVID-19 Emergency," March 20, 2022. As of May 16, 2022:
https://www.chcoc.gov/content/dual-compensation-waiver-requests-covid-19-emergency

Ogrysko, Nicole, "Agencies Can Virtually Onboard New Employees During Coronavirus Pandemic," Federal News Network, March 24, 2020. As of May 13, 2022:
https://federalnewsnetwork.com/workforce/2020/03/agencies-can-virtually-onboard-new-employees-during-coronavirus-pandemic/

OPM—*See* Office of Personnel Management.

Ortiz, B. X., D. R. McEachern, D. A. Ciani, and C.J. Chandler, "Frequency and Severity of Issues Discussed with Tier 3 Subjects," Defense Personnel and Security Research Center/Office of People Analytics, 2019, Not available to the general public.

Ortiz, X., R. Van Vechten, C. Weywadt, B. Latendresse, and B. Rapoza, "Development and Refinement of Initial Question Sets for Use in Electronic Interviews (eInterviews)," Defense Personnel and Security Research Center/Office of People Analytics, TR-20-03, 2020.

Partnership for Public Service, *Rapid Reinforcements: Strategies for Federal Surge Hiring*, Democracy Fund, October 2020. As of May 20, 2022:
https://ourpublicservice.org/wp-content/uploads/2020/10/Rapid_Reinforcements_2.pdf

Partnership for Public Service, "Fed Figures: COVID-19 and the Federal Workforce," March 9, 2021. As of May 16, 2022:
https://ourpublicservice.org/fed-figures/fed-figures-covid-19-and-the-federal-workforce/

"Personnel Vetting Reform Quarterly Progress Update FY 2022, Quarter 1," briefing slides, Performance.gov, 2022. As of August 8, 2022:
https://www.performance.gov/assets/files/Personnel_Vetting_Reform_Progress_2022_Q1.pdf

Peterson, Andrea, "Some Companies Are Tracking Workers with Smartphone Apps. What Could Possibly Go Wrong?" *Washington Post*, May 14, 2015. As of May 16, 2022:
https://www.washingtonpost.com/news/the-switch/wp/2015/05/14/some-companies-are-tracking-workers-with-smartphone-apps-what-could-possibly-go-wrong/

Piquado, Tepring, Sina Beaghley, Lisa Pelled Colabella, and Nahom M. Beyene, *Assessing the Potential for Racial Bias in the Security Clearance Process*, RAND Corporation, RR-A1201-1-v2, 2021. As of June 23, 2022:
https://www.rand.org/pubs/research_reports/RRA1201-1-v2.html

Public Law 79-404, Administrative Procedure Act, June 11, 1946.

Public Law 235, National Security Act of 1947, July 26, 1947. As of November 9, 2022:
https://www.dni.gov/index.php/ic-legal-reference-book/national-security-act-of-1947

Public Law 88-352, Civil Rights Act of 1964, July 2, 1964.

Public Law 90-202, Age Discrimination in Employment Act of 1967, December 15, 1967.

Public Law 93–579, Privacy Act of 1974, December 31, 1974.

Public Law 95-454, Civil Service Reform Act of 1978, October 13, 1978.

Public Law 101-336, Americans with Disabilities Act of 1990, July 26, 1990.

Public Law 104-191, Health Insurance Portability and Accountability Act of 1996, August 21, 1996.

Public Law 117-81, National Defense Authorization Act for Fiscal Year 2022, December 27, 2021.

Quillian, Lincoln, "Does Unconscious Racism Exist?" *Social Psychology Quarterly*, Vol. 71, No. 1, 2008.

RAND Corporation, Federal Bureau of Investigation Criminal Justice Information Services Division, and Bureau of Justice Statistics, *Comparison of Criminal-History Information Systems in the United States and Other Countries*, Bureau of Justice Statistics, April 2, 2020. As of November 29, 2022:
https://www.bjs.gov/content/pub/pdf/CCHISUSOC.pdf?utm_campaign=justinfo&utm_medi

Rigas, Michael J., "Temporary Procedures for Personnel Vetting and Appointment of New Employees During Maximum Telework Period Due to Coronavirus COVID-19," memorandum, Office of Personnel Management, March 25, 2020. As of November 9, 2022:
https://www.opm.gov/policy-data-oversight/covid-19/temporary-procedures-for-personnel-vetting-and-appointment-of-new-employees-during-maximum-telework-period-due-to-coronavirus-covid-19/

Sailors, Olivia C., "At the Nexus of Neoliberalism, Mass Incarceration, and Scientific Racism: The Conflation of Blackness with Risk in the 21st Century," *Tapestries: Interwoven Voices of Local and Global Identities*, Vol. 9, No. 1, Article 7, 2020.

Security, Suitability, and Credentialing Performance Accountability Council Program Management Office, "PAC PMO and Research and Innovation Program Overview," January 2020. As of November 14, 2022:
https://www.search.org/files/pdf/PACPMO-RAndIProgramOverview-Jan20.pdf

Serbu, Jared, "Adieu to CVR, the Platform That Taught DoD How to Act as an IT Enterprise," Federal News Network Radio, June 21, 2021. As of November 9, 2022:
https://federalnewsnetwork.com/on-dod/2021/06/
adieu-to-cvr-the-platform-that-taught-dod-how-to-act-as-an-it-enterprise/

Silver, Damon W., "5 Key Data Privacy and Security Risks That Arise When Organizations Record Job Interviews and Strategies for Mitigating Them," *National Law Review*, Vol. XII, No. 338, April 13, 2021. As of December 6, 2022:
https://www.natlawreview.com/article/5-key-data-privacy-and-security-risks-arise-when-organizations-record-job-interviews

Society for Human Resource Management, *Talent Acquisition: A Guide to Understanding and Managing the Recruitment Process*, 2016. As of June 3, 2022:
https://www.shrm.org/hr-today/trends-and-forecasting/special-reports-and-expert-views/documents/talent-acquisition-recruitment.pdf

SSC PAC PMO—*See* Security, Suitability, and Credentialing Performance Accountability Council Program Management Office.

Trump, Donald J., Executive Order 13869, "Transferring Responsibility for Background Investigations to the Department of Defense," April 29, 2019. As of November 9, 2022:
https://www.federalregister.gov/documents/2019/04/29/2019-08797/transferring-responsibility-for-background-investigations-to-the-department-of-defense

Trump, Donald J., Executive Order 39457, "Modernizing and Reforming the Assessment and Hiring of Federal Job Candidates," June 26, 2020. As of November 9, 2022:
https://www.govinfo.gov/content/pkg/FR-2020-07-01/pdf/2020-14337.pdf

U.S. Chief Information Officers Council, "CIO Council Priorities: The President's Management Agenda (PMA)," webpage, undated. As of May 16, 2022:
https://www.cio.gov/pma/

U.S. Citizenship and Immigration Services, "DHS Extends Form I-9 Requirement Flexibility," press release April 25, 2022a. As of November 30, 2022:
https://www.uscis.gov/i-9-central/covid-19-form-i-9-related-news/dhs-extends-form-i-9-requirement-flexibility-effective-may-1-2022

U.S. Citizenship and Immigration Services, "Temporary Policies Related to COVID-19," July 22, 2022b. As of August 12, 2022:
https://www.uscis.gov/i-9-central/form-i-9-related-news/temporary-policies-related-to-covid-19

U.S. Code of Federal Regulations, Title 5. As of November 14, 2022:
https://www.ecfr.gov/current/title-5

U.S. Code of Federal Regulations, Title 5, Section 213.3102, Entire executive civil service.

U.S. Code of Federal Regulations, Title 5, Section 731.101, Suitability. As of June 23, 2022:
https://www.ecfr.gov/current/title-5/chapter-I/subchapter-B/part-731

U.S. Code of Federal Regulations, Title 5, Section 731.202, Criteria for Making Suitability Determinations.

U.S. Code of Federal Regulations, Title 5, Section 2102, Parts 213 and 302.

U.S. Code of Federal Regulations, Title 18, Section 3a.11, Classification of Official Information. As of June 15, 2022:
https://www.law.cornell.edu/cfr/text/18/3a.11

U.S. Code of Federal Regulations, Title 45, Subtitle A, Subchapter A, Part 46, "Public Welfare." As of November 14, 2022:
https://www.ecfr.gov/current/title-45/subtitle-A/subchapter-A/part-46?toc=1

U.S. Code, Title 5, Section 552a, Records Maintained on Individuals.

U.S. Code, Title 5, Section 9101, Access to Criminal History Records for National Security and Other Purposes.

U.S. Code, Title 15, Section 1681, Fair Credit Reporting Act.

U.S. Code, Title 18, Chapter 119, Sections 2510–2523, Electronic Communications Privacy Act of 1986.

U.S. Code, Title 29, Chapter 22, Employee Polygraph Protection.

U.S. Department of Homeland Security, "ICE Announces Flexibility in Requirements Related to Form I-9 Compliance," press release, March 23, 2020a. As of May 13, 2022: https://www.ice.gov/news/releases/dhs-announces-flexibility-requirements-related-form-i-9-compliance

U.S. Department of Homeland Security, "ICE Announces Extension of Flexibility in Rules Related to Form I-9 Compliance," press release, May 14, 2020b. As of May 13, 2022: https://www.ice.gov/news/releases/ice-announces-extension-flexibility-rules-related-form-i-9-compliance

U.S. Department of Homeland Security, "ICE Announces Another 30-Day Extension of Flexibility in Rules Related to Form I-9 Compliance," June 16, 2020c. As of May 13, 2022: https://www.ice.gov/news/releases/ice-announces-another-30-day-extension-flexibility-rules-related-form-i-9-compliance

U.S. Department of Homeland Security, "ICE Announces Another Extension to I-9 Compliance Flexibility, No More Extensions for Employers to Respond to NOIs Served in March," press release, July 18, 2020d. As of May 13, 2022: https://www.ice.gov/news/releases/ice-announces-another-extension-i-9-compliance-flexibility-no-more-extensions

U.S. Department of Homeland Security, "ICE Announces Another Extension To I-9 Compliance," press release, August 18, 2020e. As of May 13, 2022: https://www.ice.gov/news/releases/ice-announces-another-extension-i-9-compliance-flexibility

U.S. Department of Homeland Security, "ICE Announces Extension to I-9 Compliance Flexibility," press release, September 14, 2020f. As of May 13, 2022: https://www.ice.gov/news/releases/ice-announces-extension-i-9-compliance-flexibility

U.S. Department of Homeland Security, "ICE Announces Extension to I-9 Compliance Flexibility," November 18, 2020g. As of May 13, 2022: https://www.ice.gov/news/releases/ice-announces-extension-i-9-compliance-flexibility-0

U.S. Department of Homeland Security, "ICE Announces Extension to I-9 Compliance Flexibility," press release, December 23, 2020h. As of May 13, 2022: https://www.ice.gov/news/releases/ice-announces-extension-i-9-compliance-flexibility-1

U.S. Department of Homeland Security, "ICE Announces Extension to I-9 Compliance Flexibility," press release, January 27, 2021a. As of May 13, 2022: https://www.ice.gov/news/releases/ice-announces-extension-i-9-compliance-flexibility-2

U.S. Department of Homeland Security, "ICE Announces Extension, New Employee Guidance to I-9 Compliance Flexibility," press release, March 31, 2021b. As of May 13, 2022: https://www.ice.gov/news/releases/ice-announces-extension-new-employee-guidance-i-9-compliance-flexibility

U.S. Department of Homeland Security, "ICE Announces Extension, New Employee Guidance to I-9 Compliance Flexibility," press release, May 26, 2021c. As of May 13, 2022: https://www.ice.gov/news/releases/ice-announces-extension-new-employee-guidance-i-9-compliance-flexibility-0

U.S. Department of Homeland Security, "ICE Announces Extension to New Employee Guidance to I-9 Compliance Flexibility," press release, August 31, 2021d. As of May 13, 2022: https://www.ice.gov/news/releases/ice-announces-extension-new-employee-guidance-i-9-compliance-flexibility-1

U.S. Department of Homeland Security, "ICE Announces Extension to I-9 Compliance Flexibility," press release, December 15, 2021e. As of May 13, 2022: https://www.ice.gov/news/releases/ice-announces-extension-i-9-compliance-flexibility-3

U.S. Department of Homeland Security, "ICE Announces Extension to I-9 Compliance Flexibility," press release, April 25, 2022a. As of June 23, 2022: https://www.ice.gov/news/releases/ice-announces-extension-i-9-compliance-flexibility-3

U.S. Department of Homeland Security, "I-9, Employment Eligibility Verification," November 10, 2022b. As of November 30, 2022: https://www.uscis.gov/i-9

U.S. General Services Administration, "USAccess: Identity, Credentials, and Access Management," webpage, undated. As of November 9, 2022: https://www.gsa.gov/technology/technology-purchasing-programs/usaccess-identity-credentials-and-access-management

U.S. Government Accountability Office, *Information Security: OPM Has Improved Controls, but Further Efforts Are Needed*, GAO-17-614, August 3, 2017. As of June 8, 2022: https://www.gao.gov/products/gao-17-614

U.S. Government Accountability Office, *Personnel Vetting: Actions Needed to Implement Reforms, Address Challenges, and Improve Planning*, GAO-22-104093, December 2021. As of November 9, 2022: https://www.gao.gov/assets/gao-22-104093.pdf

U.S. Merit Systems Protection Board, *Reforming Federal Hiring*, report to the President and the Congress of the United States, undated. As of February 3, 2022: https://www.mspb.gov/studies/studies/Reforming_Federal_Hiring_Beyond_Faster_and_Cheaper_224102.pdf

Vincent, James, "Amazon Delivery Drivers Have to Consent to Surveillance in Their Vans or Lose Their Jobs," *The Verge*, March 24, 2021. As of May 16, 2022: https://www.theverge.com/2021/3/24/22347945/amazon-delivery-drivers-ai-surveillance-cameras-vans-consent-form

"What Is ELSI Research?" *ELSIhub*, undated. As of June 16, 2022: https://elsihub.org/about/what-is-elsi-research

Xia, Rosanna, Howard Blume, and Luke Money, "USC, School Districts Getting 'Zoom-Bombed' with Racist Taunts, Porn as They Transition to Online Meetings," *Los Angeles Times*, March 25, 2020. As of November 14, 2022: https://www.latimes.com/california/story/2020-03-25/zoombombing-usc-classes-interrupted-racist-remarks

Zielinski, Dave, "How to Purchase an Applicant Tracking System," Society for Human Resource Management, April 12, 2021. As of November 14, 2022: https://www.shrm.org/resourcesandtools/hr-topics/talent-acquisition/pages/shrm-ats-buyers-guide-2021.aspx